LIFE, LOVE AND MARRIAGE

LIFE, LOVE AND MARRIAGE

BY

CHEIRO

GYAN

Published by

GYAN

Gyan Publishing House
5, Ansari Road
Daryaganj, New Delhi-110002
Phone: 011-47034999, 9811692060
E-mail: books@gyanbooks.com

Distribution Network
gyanbooks.com
India, USA, Canada, UK, Australia

ISBN: 978-93-6280-545-4 (HB)
First Published, 1920

2nd Impression 2024

Printed at: Gyan Press, Delhi.

LIFE, LOVE AND MARRIAGE
Author: CHEIRO

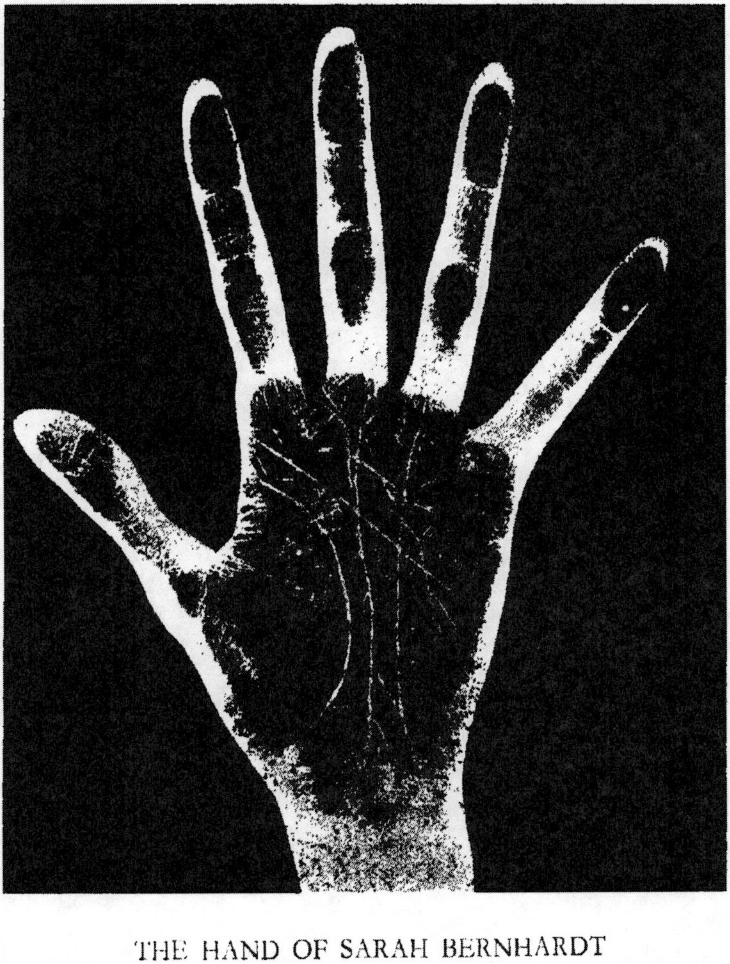

THE HAND OF SARAH BERNHARDT

LIFE, LOVE AND MARRIAGE

by

CHEIRO

(*Author of Language of the Hand, Palmistry for All, Book of Numbers, When were you Born, etc.*)

THE LONDON PUBLISHING COMPANY
62 Oxford Street, London, W.1

CONTENTS

ILLUSTRATIONS

FOREWORD

THE STUDY OF HANDS THROUGH THE CENTURIES TO THE PRESENT DAY

THE success I achieved during the twenty-one years in which I was connected with this study was, I believe, chiefly owing to the fact that, although my principal study was the lines and formation of hands, yet I did not confine myself alone to that particular page in the book of Nature. I endeavoured to study every phase of thought that can throw light on human life; consequently the very ridges of the skin, the hair found on the hands, all were used, as a detective would use a clue to accumulate evidence. I found that people were sceptical of such a study principally because the subject was not presented to them in a logical manner.

There are hundreds of facts connected with the hand of which people have rarely, if ever, heard, and I think it will not be out of place if I touch on them here. For instance, in regard to what are known as the corpuscles, Meisner, in 1853, proved that these little molecular substances were distributed in a peculiar manner in the hand itself. He found that in the tips of the fingers they were 108 to the square line, with 400 papillæ; that they gave forth certain distinct crepitations, or vibrations, and that in the red lines of the hand they were most numerous, and, strange to say, were found in straight individual rows in the lines of the palm. Experiments were made as to these vibrations, and it was proved that, after a little study, one could distinctly detect and recognise the crepitations in relation to each individual. They increased or decreased in every phase of health, thought, or excitement, and were extinct the moment death had mastered its victim. About twenty years later, experiments were made with a man in Paris, who had an abnormally acute sense of sound, Nature's compensation for want of sight, as he had been born blind. In a very short time this man could detect the slightest change or irregularity in these crepitations, and through the change, was able to tell with wonderful accuracy about how old a person was, and how near they were to illness, and even death.

The study of these corpuscles was taken up by Sir Charles Bell, who, in 1874, demonstrated that each corpuscle contained the end of a nerve fibre, and was in immediate connection with the brain. This great specialist also demonstrated that every portion of the brain was in touch with the nerves of the hand, and more particularly with the corpuscles found in the tips of the fingers and the lines of the hand.

But prejudice is a hard thing to combat, and, in consequence, a study which could render untold aid to humanity has been neglected in modern times. Yet it cannot be denied that this strange study was practised and followed by some of the greatest teachers and students of other civilisations.

Whether or no these ancient philosophers were more enlightened than we are, has long been a question of dispute, but the one point and the most important one which has been admitted is, that in those days the greatest study of mankind was man. It is, therefore, reasonable to suppose that their conclusions are more likely to be correct than those of an age like our own, famous chiefly for its implements of destruction, its warships, its dynamite, and its cannon.

This study of hands can be traced back to the very earliest, most enlightened forms of civilisation. It has been practised by the greatest minds in all those civilisations, minds that have left their mental philosophies and their monuments for us to marvel at. India, China, Persia, Egypt, Rome—all in their study of mankind have placed the greatest store in their study of the hand.

During my stay in India, I was permitted by some Brahmans (descendants of the Joshi Caste, famous from time immemorial for their knowledge in occult subjects) with whom it was my good fortune to become intimately acquainted, to examine and make extracts from an extraordinary book on this subject which they regarded as almost sacred, and which belonged to the great past of the now despised Hindustan.

It is, however, to the days of the Greek civilisation that we owe the present clear and lucid form of the study. The Greek civilisation has, in most ways, been considered the highest and most intellectual in the world, and here it is that Palmistry or Cheiromancy (from the Greek CHEIRO, the hand) grew and found favour in the eyes of those who have given us laws and philosophies that we employ to-day, and whose works are taught in all our leading colleges and schools.

It is a well-known and undisputed fact that the philosopher Anaxagoras not only taught but practised this study. We find also that Hispanus discovered on an altar dedicated to Hernes a book on Cheiromancy, written in gold letters, which he sent as a present to Alexander the Great, as "a study worthy of the attention of an elevated and enquiring mind." Instead of it being followed by the "weak-minded," we find, on the contrary, that it numbered amongst its disciples such men of learning as Aristotle, Pliny, Paracelsus, Cardamis, Albertus Magnus, the Emperor Augustus, and many others of note.

This brings us down to the period when the power of the Church was beginning to be felt outside the domain and jurisdiction of religion. It is said that the early Fathers were jealous of the influence of this old-world science. Whether this is true or not, we find that it was bitterly denounced and persecuted by the early Church. It has always been a fact that the history of any dominant creed or sect is the history of opposition to knowledge, unless that knowledge came through it. This study, therefore, the offspring of " pagans and heathens " was not even given a trial. It was denounced as sorcery and witchcraft; the devil was conjured up as the father of all such students, and the result was that, through this bitter persecution, the study was outlawed, and fell into the hands of vagrants, tramps, and gipsies. In spite of this persecution, it is interesting and significant to notice that almost the first book ever printed was a work on Palmistry, Die Kunst Ciromantia, printed in Augsburg in the year 1475.

As the student of Anatomy can build up the entire system from the examination of a single bone, so may a person by a careful study of an important member of the body such as the hand, apart from anything superstitious or even mystical, build up the entire action of the system and trace every effect back to its cause.

To-day the science of the present is coming to the rescue of the so-called superstition of the past. All over the world scientists are little by little sweeping aside prejudice and beginning to study occult questions. Perhaps the " why's and wherefores " of such things may one of these days be as easily explained as are those wireless waves of electricity that carry messages from land to land.

CHEIRO.

PART I

LOVE AND MARRIAGE

CHAPTER I

PERSONALITY

HUMAN personality is a subject of the most extraordinary fascination, and it comes directly within the province of an examination and discussion of what is called in Palmistry the Line of Heart. The heart was at one time popularly supposed to be the seat of the affections, though we know better now. It is indisputable that there is engraved upon the palm of the hand a line which gives an indication of the capacity for warm love, constancy, faithfulness, idealism, and other attractive human characteristics, just as it also shadows forth fickleness, coldness, and the incapacity to display steady affection towards one object of the opposite sex.

Human associations between the sexes are of vital importance in this life. What tremendous forces have been brought into play when passion has been aroused in the nature of a man; what multiplying events and culminating circumstances have flowed from a smile of a woman desired, or the fickleness of one who withholds her favours! When Cleopatra gave her favours to Antony, she changed the destiny of the world. "I am well lost for a smile from Ranee," cried the Emperor

Fata Raj, ruler of ancient Delhi, and rather than give up the caresses of Bel Lata, Queen of Hearts, he allowed his kingdom to be wrested from him.

When we study the humbler walks of life, we find exactly the same mysterious clash and play of personalities. Who has not met the woman or man with a mysterious power over the opposite sex! It does not lie in facial comeliness, for the greatest of lady killers is often possessed of the plainest features. Perhaps it lies in the tone of a voice, in the manner, or in an enveloping and warm " way with him," that beats down the shyness and establishes confidence with a member of the opposite sex.

Women who bring all sorts and conditions of men beneath their feet are frequently encountered in this life, yet it would be difficult for them to explain just what constitutes the secret of their domination. But for them even men of the most staid disposition have been known to throw up all the conventionalities of life, to tear down the very fabric of their business life, and destroy their own reputations. These modern Cleopatras and Catherines possess a magnetic attraction, and they are fatal companions for men.

The man who is unattractive, the woman who secretly mourns that no man ever falls at her feet, incoherent with protestations of undying affection—those indeed, who lack personality, may be inclined to think that they have been hardly treated by

Fate. But let them pause before, like Midas, they wish from the gods a gift that may prove a terrible curse, if found in excess.

In my consulting rooms, while engaged in examining hundreds of hands, I naturally came across some singular instances of men and women whose Line of Heart—the key line to the human affections—showed some remarkable deviations and developments.

I recollect on one occasion a beautiful young woman came to see me, and said, abruptly, as she laid

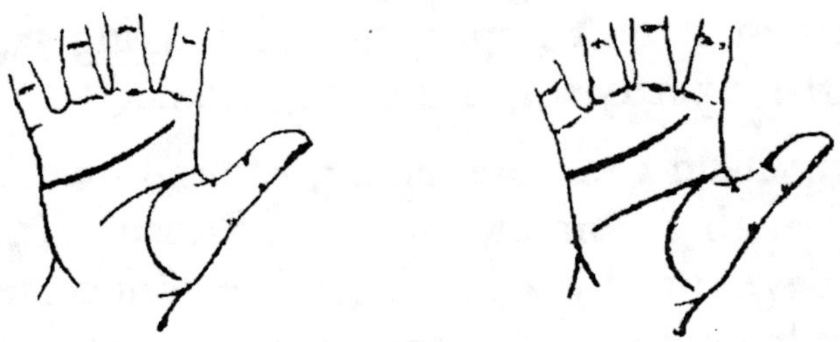

FIG 1. FIG 2.

THE LINE OF HEART RISING ON MOUNT OF APOLLO

an exquisite pair of hands upon the cushion before me :

" Cheiro, if you can indeed reveal much that is obscure, tell me why my life is such a hideous tangle ?"

I examined her palms, and I was struck by the extraordinary prominence of her Line of Heart.

Now, if you will look at the palm of your own hand, you will see this line, called also the Mensal, running across the upper part.

When the Heart Line is deeper and more powerful than the Head Line (Fig. 1) the desire for love will outweigh every other consideration.

When the Head Line is powerful (Fig. 2) such a person will be most unselfish where the affections are concerned.

It may rise from any one of several important positions: the middle of the Mount of Jupiter, to be found immediately under the first finger; between the first and second fingers; or from the Mount of Saturn, which forms a soft pad underneath the second finger. Whichever the position, it bears in a most important and striking fashion upon the capacity for love and constancy.

In the hand I was examining, I found the Line of Heart running from the Mount of Saturn. Indeed, I had never in all my professional experience found so deeply marked and characteristic a line. I knew its story—a story that could not lie, because Nature has graved these marks as the sign manual of the sex passions. When I saw other lines, indicative of a short career, stormy with misunderstandings and hectic domestic "scenes," I could "read the document" laid before me quite easily.

"Madam, you are troubled," I said.

"Oh, yes!"

"Troubled about your husband." She bowed her head. "There have been frequent scenes, recriminations, violent quarrels, and even blows."

She shuddered. I proceeded: "But the end of it all is very near."

At this, she gave a glad cry of relief, saying passionately: "Oh, Cheiro, is that indeed so! I have been so utterly miserable and unhappy."

I told her that a divorce would come within a year.

"Your husband will divorce you, and for a time you will find happiness. But I warn you there will be no abiding happiness, unless——" I paused in order to find exactly the right words to express the matter as delicately as possible. Then I went on: "Your great need, Madam, is self-control. Have you not found that always you have admirers in your life? Your husband I judge to be a cold and self-centred man, while you are endowed with a force of magnetism that must inevitably draw men to your feet."

"Cheiro," she said quietly, "you have spoken the absolute truth. Ever since I was a girl I have had lovers and admirers—even elderly men have made love to me in a manner I could not understand. At last, in order to escape from a home where I was misunderstood, I hastily allied myself with a wealthy business man, whose cold exterior I thought merely masked the absent-mindedness of the commercial type. But I soon found that marriage did not alter him. His chilly nature caused an intense sense of repulsion, and I was never happy unless we had company. It was not long before I was surrounded by lovers, although I was married. Can you wonder that I am miserable?"

I could not, for here was an instance of Ice wedding Fire—naturally the twain could never "be one flesh and one spirit." This girl had the instincts of a Cleopatra; I feared, unless she exercised the greatest self-control, that some tragedy would come into her life with such an amazing Heart Line shadowing forth its story.

Some time later I read that her husband had obtained a divorce. The case was undefended, and a marriage with the co-respondent followed. But within twelve months he had committed suicide, alleging that his wife's conduct with men had passed his endurance. Finally the lady herself became the inmate of an asylum. My warning as to self-control had not been heeded.

Let me take an opposite case.

When the Heart Line rises from a spot between the first and second fingers, it is a most favourable sign, for it indicates the calm and deep temperament that loves equably. Such a mark shows love that will not falter; I must confess that it is oftener found in the hand of a woman than of a man. This is the love that forgives all failings, and seeks to patch the "Idol of Clay," even though the Idol has fallen more than once.

While engaged in my professional work in Paris, I was waited upon by a lady of very high birth—indeed, without revealing any secret, I may record that she was descended from the proudest of the Old French Nobility. She came to me as an ordinary client, but immediately she entered I was struck by the sadness of her manner, and the sweet and pure expression of her features.

She brought with her the print of the palms of the hands of a man, but she did not tell me to whom they belonged.

"Cheiro," she said, "I want to know what the Future holds. Will you read my hands, and also these prints that I have brought."

Now, there are some marks in the human hand that are invested with a mournful fatality. If a person has the necessary knowledge, he or she may be able to struggle against any dire influences that threaten their future; but too often the knowledge is hidden or the warning unheeded.

In the hand of this lady I read a story of a marvellous and unfaltering affection, that would not be stilled or sullied, even though there was every reason why it should falter. I saw this stream flowing onward, until it suddenly came to an abrupt end—quenched by Death.

When I came to examine the hands of the print, I read there the sequel—for love in this case was tempestuous and sweeping, ending with the suddenness of the sensualist. I did not doubt—and a few words confirmed my expectations—that this was the husband.

"Madam, you have wonderful capacity for

affection; I am sorry that it is poured out upon one who is not able to return it. Your husband's nature is fiery and passionate, but when love ends with him, it can never be re-kindled."

She repeated my words with a mournful cadence: "It can never be rekindled!" Then, like a person shaking herself from an evil dream, she cried passionately: "I do not, I will not believe you, Cheiro! Oh, I have loved my husband through evil and good report, through misunderstandings and open infidelity. Again and again I have forgiven him. Surely, surely, such love as mine must meet with its reward. He must realise its worth at last."

I could only remain silent, and after a little while the lady continued:

"I will tell you all. I have just found out that he is carrying on an intrigue with Mdlle. ——" She mentioned the name of a very celebrated Parisian dancer now dead, whose name was then a household word all over the world. "He is spending all his time and thousands of pounds upon her. It is too much!"

She wept bitterly and I begged her to be tranquil, advising her to steel her mind to the realisation that her husband *could not* be faithful, and would never be so. I felt that my words were idle, for I knew that this wonderful love of hers would continue, even though her heart was broken.

Some months later, I saw in the leading Parisian

papers, a paragraph announcing the death of Madame——, my caller. From a friend I learned that she had died of a malady that had puzzled the most eminent physicians. She had faded out of life, despite change of climate and all the attentions that wealth could give. A broken heart is not a "disease" to be inscribed upon a death certificate.

In Figs. 3 and 4, I show the Heart Line rising right under the base of the first finger (Fig. 3) and also under the base of the second finger (Fig. 4)

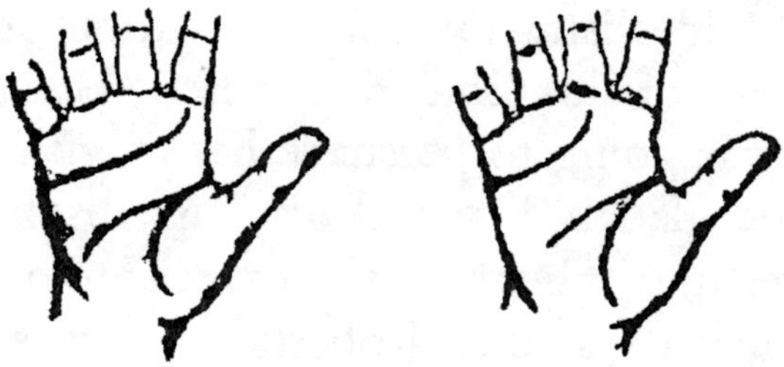

FIG 3. FIG 4.
THE LINE OF HEART

In the first case, the man *or the woman* will lay down the law in all matters concerning the affections and the home. Mr. W. E. Gladstone had a Heart Line of this character.

In the second case, the Line of Heart shows a placid, almost fatalistic state of the affection—the life partner who is only too happy to sacrifice himself or herself for the beloved.

When the Heart Line rises on the outside of the Mount of Jupiter, or from the top of the Mount, it denotes the blind enthusiast in love—the man or woman who cares not what the voice of envy or slander may say of the beloved; nothing will shake the unreasoning love that sets the object of it upon a pedestal. No wonder that Fate plays some strange tricks with lovers, when, as in the case I am about to relate, an idealist meets a woman incapable of the same overwhelming feelings.

I remember being visited by a young gentleman who told me that he was going to be married, and wished me to read his hand. As he was a highly-strung, sensitive man, with a marked characteristic for blind idealistic love, I was curious to know something of his intended wife. He told me that he was going to persuade her to visit me, and would be glad if I would give an absolutely impartial reading of her hands. I agreed to do so.

In a few days Miss Roberts—this was not her name, but it disguises a lady who achieved some fame as a musical comedy actress—fluttered in. I found her a shallow and vapid creature, obviously incapable of any real love, and extremely fickle in all things. It was astounding that such a common and changeable woman should have engrossed the affections of this high-minded and gifted youth.

When I saw the young man again, he asked me eagerly if I had read the lady's hand. I said, "Yes."

"Then, Cheiro," he cried, with sparkling eyes and animated face, "tell me that the future holds a happy marriage for us, for I love that woman to the point of distraction. Isn't she wonderful—almost a divine creature?"

What could I say? I hated to wound his feelings; on the other hand, I felt that a solemn duty had to be discharged.

As tactfully as I knew how, I explained the differences in their temperaments—that while his love was idealistic, and covered her with a soft robe of perfection, *her* love was faint and fickle, and must soon come to an end. Moreover, seeing that admiration was the breath of life to her, it was obvious that all too soon misunderstandings and unhappiness would follow in the train of marriage.

He listened with downcast face and sullen eyes.

"Cheiro, I don't believe you," he said when I had finished. "No, you are wrong! You cannot realise what that woman is, and what she means to me. If a whole college of cardinals advised me not to marry her, I should go on with it."

I made one last effort.

"Be warned," I said; and I added solemnly, "I see not only danger, but *death* if you persist."

He laughed in the strength of his incredulity, and rushed on to his Fate. The wedding was much commented upon, owing to his extravagant display. Within a year the couple had parted; before another had waned the separated husband, heart-broken and adrift, had poisoned himself.

Such a marriage was bound to end in disaster, although such a love—so blind and so trusting—if bestowed upon a woman worthy of it, would result in one of those idealistic unions that are, as the poet says, " a faint presage of the bliss of those who walk in light."

But alas! how rarely does Like meet Like, or the affinity find a mate. But a knowledge of these facts, and they are scored upon the palm of the hand, must be a wonderful help in preventing those disastrous unions that are foredoomed to misery and crowd the divorce court.

There are instances, of course, where this idealistic love has been crowned in striking fashion. I had the pleasure of reading the hand of Mr. Gladstone in the very early part of my career. On the hand of the grand old statesman was stamped the seal of idealistic affection; from a glance that I took at Mrs. Gladstone's palm I noted a similar sign. Everybody is aware of the unwavering and almost reverent affection that Mrs. Gladstone had for her great husband, while he returned it with a courtly and chivalrous love that was very beautiful.

It may be interesting to put on record how I came in contact with Mr. Gladstone, for it was, naturally, when he was well advanced in years.

During one of my visits to Richmond Terrace, the great explorer, H. M. Stanley, suggested, to my astonishment, that I should meet Gladstone.

"Mrs. Stanley will arrange it for you, if you like," he said.

His wife agreed, and sat down at once and wrote the letter.

By return of post came one of Gladstone's

famous postcards, offering me an appointment for the following day at Hawarden Castle. That night I took the train to Chester, and the next day at three o'clock I kept my appointment.

It was a hot day in August. Mr. Gladstone had, the day before, made what was, I believe, his last public speech, when he addressed the Horticultural Society of Chester.

Mrs. Gladstone met me in the hall and my heart sank as she said that Mr. Gladstone was so fatigued that she must refuse to have him disturbed on any pretext.

I told her how sorry I was to hear of Mr. Gladstone's indisposition, but that I should be happy to come again from London at any time he wished. Then I turned to go.

At this moment the " grand old man " opened the door of his study.

" My dear, is that the gentleman who has an appointment with me at three o'clock ?"

" Yes, but you must not see any one to-day," replied Mrs. Gladstone.

" But, my dear," he pointed out, " this man has come all the way from London at my invitation. He is a friend of the Stanley's, and it will interest me to see him."

" Sir," I said, " please do not consider me. I will come another day, when you are feeling better."

" I will see you now," he answered, and then,

with a sad tone in his voice, he added, "I may never be better than I am to-day."

We walked into his well-known study, and he motioned me to a seat by the window. One of my own books lay on a table by his side, and I saw to my surprise that he had evidently determined to know something about my work before he met me. I heard later that this was his invariable custom—the reading up beforehand of any subject on which he was about to be interviewed.

But there was a still greater surprise in store, and also an example of his wonderful memory.

" I have been told that you are the son of ——," he said. " Your father had the same love of mathematics that I have. We have corresponded many times on difficult problems—here is one which he worked out about twelve years ago, and which has interested me many times since."

As he spoke he unrolled several sheets of paper, covered with calculations in algebraical figures in my father's handwriting.

" Is your father still living ?" he asked.

" No, sir," I answered ; " he passed away only a short time ago."

The gentleness and kindness of this wonderful man—this man who had so often swayed the destinies of nations—whose intelligence was acknowledged even by his enemies—completely conquered my nervousness, and, astonished at my own confidence, I plunged at once into my subject. At

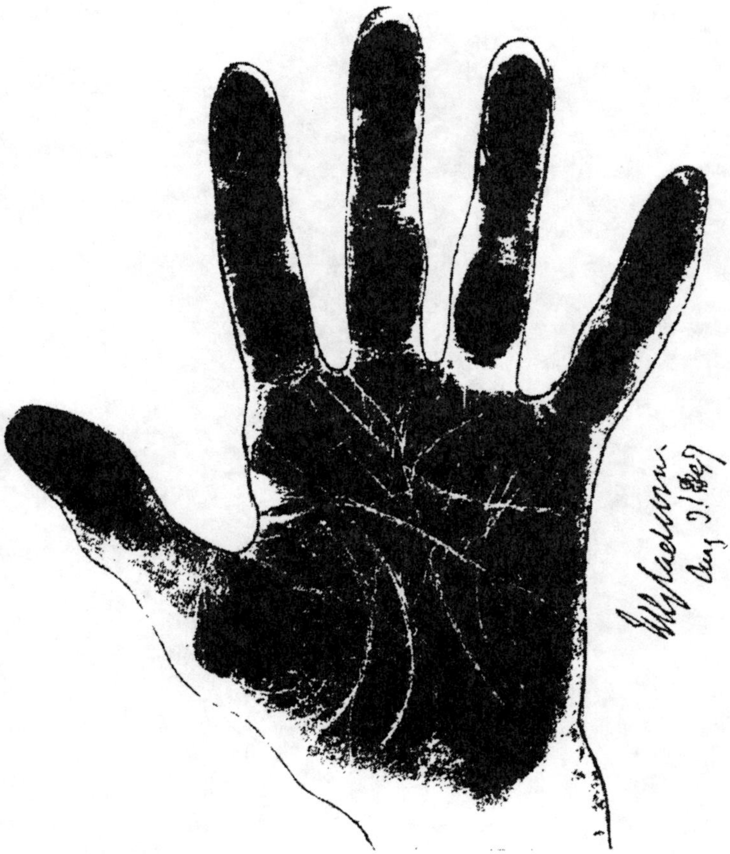

THE HAND OF WILLIAM EWART GLADSTONE

first I rapidly explained the theories associated with the study, and backed them up with some impressions of hands showing heredity and other signs.

I need not go more fully into the lines of his hands; suffice it to say that his Heart Line cut right across the Mount of Apollo, starting at the very centre of the ball of the first finger. It was a splendid line from my point of view, and I need not remind my readers that the "Darby and Joan" affection existing between Mr. and Mrs. Gladstone was well-known during their lifetime.

It is almost as good when the Line of Heart starts from the centre of this Mount of Apollo, but in such a case it denotes less of sex in the ideals of the subject. A splendid example of this is seen on the hands of that most wonderful French woman, the divine Sarah Bernhardt.

One evening, a gentleman asked if I would drive out with him and meet a lady whose hands he thought would be of great interest to me. I agreed, and together we went to a house standing in a large garden near St. John's Wood. I had been made to promise to ask no questions, but I must confess I was somewhat anxious when, after what appeared to me a considerable time, the door at the end of a corridor opened, and a lady, with a heavy black lace mantilla covering her head and face, came towards me and held her hands out under a shaded electric light.

What hands they were! From my point of view—of lines and marks—they completely fascinated me.

After my description of the pathway of brilliancy and success—the glory of the conquest—the triumphs, and also the trials of the successful, I painted the ending of the day, the burning out one by one of the lamps of life, the slow levelling process of the hills of hope and ambition, and something else, that seemed like a tragedy—and the end.

The white hands were drawn away, great sobs came from under the veil, until suddenly it was thrown back, and those wonderful eyes of the great Sarah looked straight into mine.

It is not my part in these sketches to tell of my own feelings, or of my emotions, but I must admit that, at this early stage of my unusual career, I felt a flush of gratitude to the study that had brought me so close to the divine Sarah Bernhardt, especially as, in the sweetest of voices my young ears had ever known, she murmured over and over again in French, "It is the most wonderful thing I have ever known—wonderful, wonderful, wonderful!"

Before I left I took an impression of her hand in plaster, which I published some years ago in my well-known book, "Cheiro's Language of the Hand." (*See* Frontispiece).

As its main characteristics are most decided and

clear, a short explanation may, I think, be of interest to my readers.

In the first place, the shape of a hand to the student of such things should surely tell as much as the shape of the limbs of a horse to a judge of thoroughbreds.

People with square-shaped, heavy hands, with square-looking, blunt fingers, are found to be methodical, solid, materialistic in their thoughts and actions, whereas those with plump, rounded hands and pointed fingers are found to be impulsive, excitable, artistic, and so forth.

Madame Bernhardt's hands belonged to the latter, and not to the former description.

Now, glancing at the lines (which are the indication of the mentality), it has equally been found that all persons who have straight decided-looking lines have strong decided personalities, which stamp all they undertake with their will power, precision and purpose. Some may have only one line straight and clearly indicated, and all the others slightly marked or wavering ; they will be found to be decided in purpose in whatever that line represents.

In Madame Bernhardt's case, however, nearly all the principal lines are exceptionally clear and straight, and in such a case one would find that the owner must mark all she would undertake with an unmistakable personality of her own ; Madame Bernhardt's career is too well known for me to draw examples of this from the various things she has undertaken, but it is admitted that even her sculpture has always been as decided in its character as her dramatic power has been in another branch of art.

The centre horizontal line, lying across the middle of the palm, is called the Line of Head or Mentality.

When found, as it is in her case, straight and clear, it indicates a strongly marked mentality, an active determined will—and by lying so evenly across the palm, great versatility of talent in all which that mental will may dictate to its owner to undertake.

For our present purpose, it is important to notice that the Heart Line rises very low on the Mount of Jupiter and about the centre. Here is no strong sexual passion, as seen in the Saturnian Heart Lines, but an intense depth of friendship for man and woman alike. The Heart Line is seldom found so low on the Mount.

To understand the mystery of Personality, therefore, we must grasp something of the essential facts of the Occult. Men and women are born under various planetary influences, and the tale of it is writ upon the hand. The mercurial man is hot and cold, changeable as the April weather, sometimes glowing, but sometimes gloomy. The saturnine person will plot and plan, scheme and contrive, he is wily and diplomatic. Some are influenced inordinately by malignant powers; others are happily guided by beneficent. As we pass through life, and are brought into contact with various individuals, we feel the different forces. From some we want to retreat; others attract us. In no human relationship are these forces so potent as in marriage, when the sexes mingle, and, for weal or woe, the dual life flows on.

The shorter the Line of Heart is on the hand, the less the higher sentiments of the affection make themselves manifest.

When the Line of Heart is found in excess—namely, extremely long—it denotes a terrible tendency towards jealousy, and this is alarmingly increased if the Line of Head on the same hand is very sloping towards the Mount of the Moon. In such a case the imagination will run away with itself where jealousy is concerned.

When the Line of Heart is found curving downwards at the base of the Mount of Jupiter, it tells of a strange fatality in that person, great disappointment in love, and even with those they trust in friendship. They seem to lack perception, in knowing whom to love. Their affections are nearly always misplaced or never returned.

These people have, however, as a rule, wonderfully kind, affectionate dispositions. They have little pride about whom they love, and they generally marry beneath their station in life.

A Line of Heart made up like a chain, or by a

crowd of little lines running into it, denotes flirtations and inconstancy in the love nature, and seldom has any lasting affection.

A Line of Heart from Saturn, in holes or links like a chain, especially when it is broad, denotes an absolute contempt for the opposite sex. It is one of the signs of mental degeneration as far as love is concerned.

When this line is pale and broad, without any depth, it denotes a nature blasé and indifferent, with no depth of affection.

When very low down on the hand, almost touching the Line of Head, the heart will always interfere with the affairs of the head.

When it lies very high on the hand and the space is narrowed only by the Head Line being abnormally high and out of its place, it indicates the reverse of the above, and that the affairs of the heart are ruled by the head. Such persons are extremely calculating in all matters of love.

When only one deep straightened line is found across the hand from side to side, the two Lines of Head and Heart appearing to blend together, this denotes an intensely self-concentrated nature. If they love, they unite it with all the forces of their mind, and if they put their mind on any subject, they throw their whole heart and soul into whatever it may be.

These people are also terribly headstrong and self-willed in all they do. They do not seem to know what fear means in any sense—they are dangerous lovers and husbands, for they will stop at nothing, if their blood is once roused.

They are also dangerous to themselves. They rush blindly into danger, and they usually meet with terrible accidents and injuries, and very often suffer a violent death. I shall deal with this type in a later chapter.

When the Line of Heart commences with a fork, one branch on Jupiter and the other between the first and second fingers, it is an excellent sign of a well-balanced, happy, affectionate disposition, and a good promise of great happiness in all matters of affection.

When the Line of Heart is very thin and with no branches, it denotes coldness and want of heart.

A broken Heart Line is a certain sign that some terrible tragedy in the affections will at some time or other overwhelm the subject.

It may not often be found nowadays, but I have seen it in some few cases, and these persons never recovered the loss of the loved one, or ever had love in their lives again.

CHAPTER II

LOVE'S HYPOCRITES

THERE are a great many marriages that seem, to the world, to be happy. Indeed, the unthinking may say, " Mr. and Mrs. So-and-So are quite an ideal couple. They never seem to wrangle, but jog along quite happily." But that is the judgment of those who can of necessity only judge from the outside. Men and women, when united in holy matrimony, will often contrive to hide their real feelings from the prying eyes of the world.

Too often, in my consulting room, the veil would be lifted and the Truth revealed.

" Cheiro," I have heard men sigh, " I'm wretchedly unhappy in my domestic life. But you must understand that my wife is a good wife in the best domestic sense. Yes, she is quite all right! But I don't love her, and I realise that we are getting on each other's nerves. Where is it all going to end?"

Or perhaps a wife would confide:

" I have no real happiness in my married life, for love seems dead. What a prospect! To be tied to the same man year after year, and just exist like a vegetable."

Too often the sequel is ultimately found in a sudden separation, caused by the wife discovering that the husband has consoled himself with a hidden mistress, revealed by some accident or possibly by design on his part.

That people can be happy in marriage is obvious, for there are happy examples to be found here and there. The reason why *more* couples are not happy is because, too often, they wilfully shut their eyes before the fatal step is taken. It is a bitter truth that Love is Blind—passion too often blinds the eyes to obvious facts.

I have seen many examples of what I will call Love's Hypocrites. By this I mean those who preserve to the outside world the affectation of being the model husband, or it may be wife, but in reality conceal a domestic tragedy that sometimes blazes out into sudden public notice.

Consider the Line of Heart when it rises on the Mount of Saturn—see Fig. 4.

For where an Apollo line points to influences at once beneficent and kindly, giving the love that is indeed " stronger than Death and that many waters cannot quench," here we get selfishness, cynicism, reservations, and a lack of demonstration. Woe to the woman who is tied to a man with this mark in excess over others, for she will be the wife of one who, through self-interest and a love of proprieties, turns a smiling face to the world and appears to be the model husband. Yet in secret Self rules, the domestic atmosphere is chill with reserve, and Cynicism darts forth its venomed tongue.

Curious, is it not, that these types are often the most persistent of lovers. It is not the hot urge of passion that sweeps them on, but an iron determination to bring a scheme to fruition. If it means winning a woman, that woman must be won. Gautier, in his incomparable picture of Rosie, the crushed wife, has shown that Louis wins her "with a cold-blooded persistence that wore out all his rivals, not because of any heat of passion, but through the chill calculation that marked her down as a desirable mate." He won, though it cost him a human life and the breaking down of another's fortune.

I shall deal elsewhere with the hand of the criminal, but in connection with the foregoing I must relate a very interesting case that came under my notice.

A caller in my consulting room appeared to the outward eye to be a highly-respectable, well-dressed gentleman of middle age. His brow was broad; his eyes alight with intelligence; his voice was emphatic and as one accustomed to be obeyed. I was particularly struck with his Line of Heart, which rose right out of Saturn, the mount of this name being extraordinarily developed.

His manner, though courteous, was off-hand, and he indicated plainly that he did not entertain much opinion of my power to reveal the Past, explain the Present, or unveil the Future. In fact he remarked :

"Now, Cheiro, I have but little belief in this nonsense called palmistry. However, say what you will," and he threw himself back in his chair.

"Then why have you troubled to come to see me ?"

"A fair question !" He paused and then added : "Tell me if I am married, and if so, whether my wife is happy ?" I looked again at the menacing sign of Saturn engraved on his hand, whence his Line of Heart took its rise. At the same time an overwhelming sense of repulsion invaded my psychic being—an instinctive desire to escape contact with this cynical character. I found words pouring from my lips—hardly dictated by Reason, but most certainly inspired by an occult understanding of this "case."

"Your wife is intensely unhappy. Her individuality is crushed ; her nature is slowly being suffocated. You are what is called a model husband—in fact, the world acclaims you as such. You never argue with her, never storm, never 'permit yourself to have scenes.' Yet slowly, but surely, your cynical tongue and icy correctness is killing her spirit."

I had got thus far, when he sprang to his feet with a wild, almost frightened expression on his face.

"Cheiro," he breathed, and looked round half

fearfully, "how—how do you know all this. Oh, I see," his expression changed and his voice flicked like a whip, "my dear wife has paid you a visit and told you all about 'her charming husband.' What an ass I am not to have thought of that before!"

I assured him that the idea was unthinkable and that I did not even know his name. He sat down again, speaking in a more natural way.

"Pardon me, if I have misjudged you. But—what you said is true to the life. Yes, I am regarded as a model husband. I won my young wife in the face of opposition—from her family, from the man to whom she was engaged—ha! ha!" He uttered a mirthless laugh. "I swept him like a dead leaf from my path, and won her!"

"You mean that she became your wife."

"Yes," he continued, in a musing tone; "she became my wife. But ever since I have been consciously living with a stranger. Oh, you can well believe that I put forth all the strength of my will to break down the barrier between us—that reserve that hid her real self. I used craft, threats of a character that could be veiled by seeming kindness. I heaped gifts upon her, I tried to wear out her patience. She remained obedient, submissive—yet I knew in my soul that I did not possess her."

"Then my reading was correct?" I asked.

"Yes, and what will the end be?"

I hesitated. It is a solemn matter to unveil the

Future, even in the most limited degree, to any fellow creature. But writ upon the hand are certain signs that cannot be disregarded and which must be read in conjunction with others. I saw that this man's life was rushing forward to a fearful climax, and I judged that his imperious nature, tormented and thwarted by his domestic problem, would come to a violent and jarring end.

"The truth, Cheiro," he said impatiently.

I told him that I believed a climax in his affairs was approaching within six months, and advised him to use the utmost caution—to go away if the strain became intolerable, and to avoid any dispute with his wife.

Time passed rapidly away, and this particular case, under the stress of my daily exacting task of seeing so many people, had ebbed completely from my mind.

I was just turning gratefully to my evening rest, worn out after an exacting day, when my secretary announced a lady. I said abruptly that it was past five, and that he knew it was my invariable rule to admit no clients after that hour. But the caller, I was told, was pressing. Finally, moved by an impulse, I said that I would see her.

There entered a tall and very striking-looking lady, with a clear cut face—a cameo of natural sweetness. I thought I discerned a film of sorrow in the violet eyes, and an expression of hardly mastered grief that had compressed her lips. She sat down and spoke without any preliminaries.

"Cheiro, I am going away from England to-morrow—probably never to return. But before I go I have a mission to fulfil."

Opening a bag, she brought out a small note-book. Turning back the leaves, she showed me an entry in the form of a diary note:

"June 16—Saw Cheiro to-day. He told me the truth with regard to myself and E. He thinks that the end will be violent; can I save myself from myself?"

After I had read this entry, it suddenly flashed into my mind that it referred to the man who had called, and upon whose hand I had seen the abnormal development of the Mount of Saturn. I looked again at my caller—she was in widow's weeds.

"Yes," she said, as if reading my thoughts, "he is dead, Cheiro. He took an overdose of medicine—at least, that is what the jury found—but just before he died, he was able to gasp out a message to the effect that this book was to be taken to you."

I must not reveal all I heard from the lips of this lady concerning her married life: her confidence was sacred. Sufficient to record that it was a martyrdom. Her heart belonged to the lover that she had lost—lost, as I now knew, through the crafty machinations of the dead man who had stooped to lies, trickery, and the basest slander to gain his end. Not without reason have we embodied in our expressions that most significant one, "A *saturnine* person!" I looked at the hand of the lady, and found, as I had expected, a line of Heart that showed pure, steadfast, sacrificing love. Moreover, I found evidence that at a not very distant date that love would be crowned. It was—under dramatic circumstances.

While fulfilling a very successful Paris season the following year, I received two visitors—a lady and a gentleman. To my astonishment the woman turned out to be my lady client; the other was her lost lover, now her husband, whom she had encountered in Paris.

"I am perfectly happy, Cheiro," she said.

Since that day I have often heard from both husband and wife; indeed, I number them among my dearest friends. I think I can say with regard to them that theirs is a perfect union—the welding of body *and* spirit into one harmonious perfection of unity.

Love's hypocrities—those unfortunate individuals who mask a cold heart with a smooth and even exterior—are not confined to men. The woman dominated by Saturn is a potent creature of mischief-making possibilities. Such a one will, to serve her own ends, simulate love and passion with astounding persistence, deceiving a husband or lover, while all the time working for entirely selfish ends.

Among adventuresses will be found, again and again, the Line of Heart rising well under the base of the Mount of Saturn. One of the most dramatic cases that came under my notice bears on this very point.

I had a visit one day from a young man. He was very rich, and rather simple. He told me that he was engaged to a young lady, and nothing would satisfy him but that I must read her hands as well.

"Cheiro, she is the most wonderful woman in the whole world! As pure as an angel, and as affectionate as any man could wish. I'm dying with impatience for the wedding-day."

All very proper, of course, for a young man when in love; but naturally I reserved my own opinion until I had had a sight of the damsel and had examined her hand.

In due course she arrived. I had stipulated that the interview should be in the absence of the lover, for I like to concentrate on a case, and seldom tolerate a third party present. The girl was certainly a magnificent creature, with a wealth of Titian hair and a queenly carriage. Her features were good, though a trifle too pronounced, while I fancied that I detected a hint of cynicism in her lips.

Her hands were well-shaped, indicating good physical health, and a masterful will. But when I turned with interest to the Line of Heart, I saw at once that I was in the presence of an abnormal woman.

Her Line of Heart rose immediately under the base of the Mount of Saturn. It was a very short line, and my experience has proved that where this line is short, it indicates an inability to feel natural affection; in fact, *Self* is the first and last and only consideration.

As I examined the woman's Line of Heart, I saw that here was a characteristic love hypocrite—one who for personal motive would pretend to feel passion. The case intrigued me, for the girl was certainly a most fascinating woman of the world, and as I proceeded, I got the impression that she was a natural adventuress.

I noticed on her hand that marriage meant a terrific tangle—a complication that led not only to the divorce court, but to other courts. Certainly there was danger ahead for the simple young man, if he married this handsome young woman.

I told her that she was very clever, a born schemer, and that her ability to look after Number One was very pronounced. She laughed at my guarded hints.

"So you think I'm an adventuress, eh? Well, I can watch over my interests right enough, and that's what matters."

After some more conversation she took her leave, and the next day her lover came to see me.

I tried to prepare him, as tactfully as possible, for my opinion. But when I explained that I felt that the love was all on his side, and that he should use the greatest caution, he grew very angry and would not listen. I let him go; for experience has taught me that it is useless to argue with a person in love. I knew that soon his eyes would be opened, and probably in dramatic fashion.

The sequel lies before me as I write this, in the form of a newspaper cutting. I suppress the name, because the young man is still living. Briefly, he married the woman, only to discover that she had committed bigamy. After the "marriage," she proceeded to wrest from the man she called her husband all his property, by tales of speculation, by veiled threats, or by wheedling him. She pretended the greatest admiration and passion for him, and he believed her—until one day he accidentally discovered a letter written to her paramour. In it she had stated: "The silly fool is still my slave, and will remain under my thumb while there is anything left."

The police court charge revealed amazing depravity on the part of this Saturnine woman. She was an adept at entangling men and then robbing them.

"She is without pity or remorse," one detective said, when describing her, and added: "When a young girl, she robbed her mother of everything."

How strikingly this bore out my diagnosis of her case. A hypocrite in love, she could simulate the most tender as well as the most fiery phases of passion, thus leading men to their ruin.

CHAPTER III

FATAL LOVES

FATAL loves! A fit subject indeed for melodrama, or the writer of highly coloured fiction.

But it must not be forgotten that in the world of Reality in which we live, the love that leads to Death is too often forced upon our notice. The columns of the newspaper mirror Life as it is, in sharp contrast with existence as seen by Imagination; again and again the heading, "A Love Tragedy," or, "Lover Kills Himself and his Beloved," forces itself upon our notice.

Love is indeed a gift of the gods, but when it glows with an excess of Passion, then it becomes an instrument to work destruction. Reason is obscured; control is flung to the winds; in the heat of madness engendered by Passion, crime is committed.

There are many felons' graves in the grim precincts of our great prisons, where the occupants moulder after "Judgment of Death" has been pronounced upon them and executed by the gallows. But none enshrine sadder stories than of those who have come to their end for a crime of "love"—murderers, because they have loved so intemperately that they have even called in Death to be their accomplice.

Men and women are heedless in love when the divine fire illuminates them and turns existence into a roseate garden. Friends may utter a warning that such a man or woman is unsuitable, or even dangerous; the very fact that "love is blind" anticipates the answer: "What you say *may* be true, but even if it were, I care not!" Love laughs at difficulties from which Reason starts in a panic. Alas, too often, Time adjusts the perspective, and then perhaps it is too late to remedy the evil.

One of the most striking illustrations of these fatal loves was illustrated by the life and death of Harriet Lane, whose hand was examined by a rather noted cheiromancer of her day—in the seventies—who made a note at the time of what he found written in her palm in those lines that cannot lie.

I should explain that when the Line of Heart is found curving downwards at the base of the Mount of Jupiter, it speaks of a strange fatality attached to that person. (No. 7 in Fig. 5.)

It indicates with unerring accuracy that such a person will experience the deepest disappointment and tragedy in love; while giving a steadfast love themselves, the return will be treachery and cruelty, and under certain circumstances, Death!

Harriet Lane was a young prepossessing girl, who, one day, met a handsome man. His real

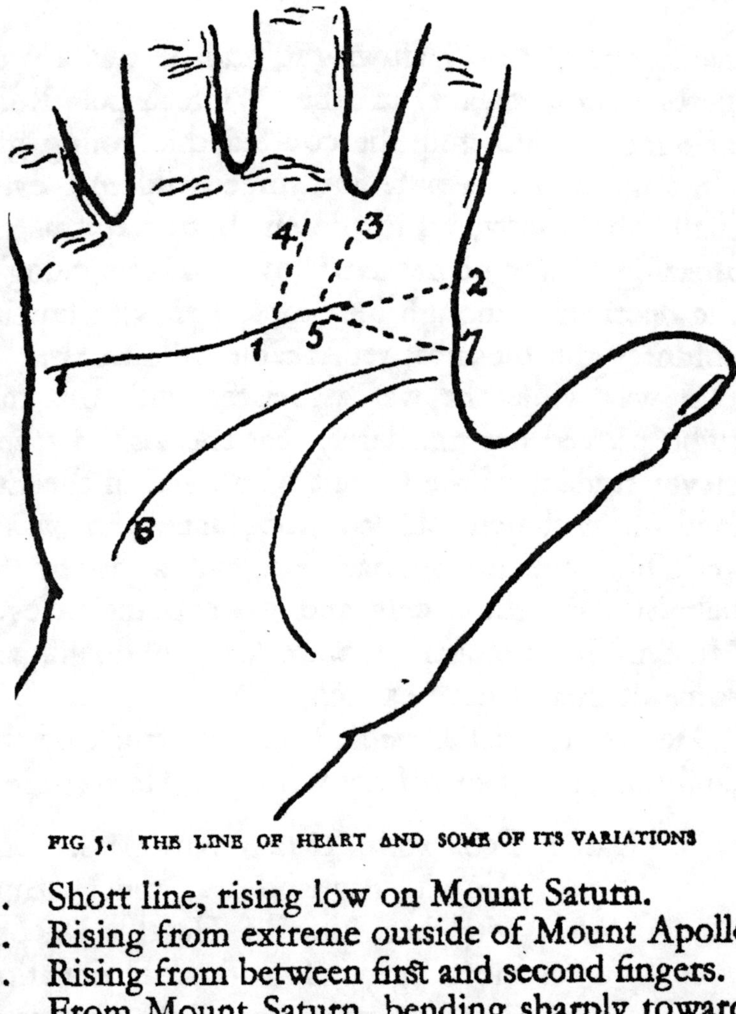

FIG 5. THE LINE OF HEART AND SOME OF ITS VARIATIONS

1. Short line, rising low on Mount Saturn.
2. Rising from extreme outside of Mount Apollo.
3. Rising from between first and second fingers.
4. From Mount Saturn, bending sharply towards Head Line.
5. From base of Mount Saturn.
6. Very sloping Head Line—running away from Heart Line—shows jealousy in a bad hand, or uncontrolled imagination concerning the loved one in a good hand.
7. Heart Line curving below Mount Apollo.

name was Henry Wainwright, and he was a prosperous brushmaker in the Whitechapel Road, London. With guile he courted this young girl, although he had a wife and three children; eventually she discovered his deceit, but such was the amazing power of her fatal love that she clung to the deceiver, although he treated her with cruelty, coldness and the most remarkable callousness.

It was while she was associated with this man (who proved her murderer) that she visited a very clever student of the Occult who lived in the East End—a withered old cosmopolitan who was a veritable human enigma. He had a hobby for palmistry and the occult, and was extremely clever. Most of his predictions were written down, and some of them I have examined.

He saw Harriet Lane and he was struck by that fatal line upon which I am writing. He recorded:

> "Date: Feb. 10th, 1872: Saw Mrs. Percy King to-day and was much struck with her Line of Heart. Uncommon signs of a *fatal* termination. Tried to warn her, then discovered she had just been married."

It should be explained that Wainwright married Harriet Lane under a false name, and she lived under the name of King until September, 1874, when she vanished. What happened was that Wainwright, tired of the expensive liason, shot her and buried the remains in his warehouse. His arrest took place a year later, and his execution on December 21st, 1875, in the yard of Old Newgate.

Now, it is a remarkable fact that this young woman was warned by several people that "King" was a bad character, and that he would be her ruin. Yet through all the unkindness and the deceit persisted that unquenchable love that refused to be killed. It lived on, indeed, until the dark hour when Wainwright turned murderer, and struck down the gentle creature who, three days before her death, had seized a pen and wrote:

> "Dearest,—I am sorry you were cross with me. But whatever you do or say I shall love you just the same. Nothing can alter my feelings. I shall always be your devoted slave."

This same line also denotes with wonderful accuracy an absence of *pride* in Love. Let me give an illustration that came under my notice while I was enjoying a very successful season in New York.

I should explain that when I first went to America I met with opposition from one of the most influential of the newspapers. I was told that I must submit to a rigorous test of my powers. If I shirked it, I might as well turn round and take the next boat back to London; if I succeeded, "my fortune was made." I have never failed to face a challenge, so I accepted.

I was given a number of prints of hands, and

without being told anything about the people to whom they belonged, I was requested to tell what I could about them. I concentrated all my will upon the test and I succeeded in a fashion that won unstinted praise. The next morning the New York papers carried full-page stories concerning "The wonderful Cheiro," and my hotel was besieged with intending clients

Among the callers was a young lady, whose father I knew by repute as one of the wealthiest of American Kings of Commerce, and whose wife was a leader of the New York Four Hundred—or Smart Set.

While I was examining the hands of this young lady, I was struck by the Line of Heart and its position. I saw that it meant either a fatal passion of love, or a love without pride—that is, the affection that does not hesitate to stoop. But from certain indications, I came to the conclusion that my caller had made a secret marriage and had wedded some man far below her station in life.

"Shall I tell you everything?" I said to her.

She hesitated for a moment and then answered bravely:

"Yes, Cheiro, I know that I can trust you. Let me know everything."

"You are married, and have been for some months. Your husband is in a very humble walk of life, and I think in some way connected with your father's business. For certain reasons you have debated whether you should tell your parents. You cannot make up your mind."

She grew very agitated.

"It is true what you say. I—I am likely to become a mother, and have been distracted to know what to do. I have been married for eight months to one of the draughtsmen in my father's steel works. What shall I do, Cheiro?"

I was perplexed, for her hand indicated hard times in store. Yet I was sure that all would turn out well in the end.

"Tell your parents. There will be a scene, and you may have to leave home. But all will come right eventually."

I was on the point of leaving America, many months later, when I received a visit from a handsome young couple. I recognised the girl who had called upon me before, and she introduced her husband. But it was not necessary for them to tell me that they were married. Soon after I had told the girl that she was secretly married, she had disclosed the fact to her parents. There had been a terrific domestic storm, that leaked into the papers, with the consequent flambuoyant publicity common to America. Her father turned her out of doors and dismissed the husband from his works. The man obtained another situation, and they lived happily in the humblest circumstances.

But the dramatic event was this.

The husband was an inventor. He perfected a

process of vital importance in the manufacture of steel. Unaware of the inventor's identity, the father-in-law opened negotiations in order to acquire the rights of the process, and offered the inventor a junior partnership in his firm. When the negotiations were complete he found that he had accepted his son-in-law! Struck by the dramatic situation, he behaved with good grace, and a reconciliation took place. The girl's line of "love without pride" had been fully justified.

What can be more fascinating and instructive than to observe the various forms of love in human life! It is a common mistake to suppose that all love is similar, for the truth is that there are many varied forms. When men and women come together in the intimate and sacred bonds of marriage, the Law and the Church blindly assumes that there is an equality, and upon this is founded the idea of a "happy union." But the human hand tells another story! It bears the impress of those mysterious Planetary influences that mould character, colour personality, and invest a man and woman with attractiveness or repulsion.

That the Creator intended all men and women to be happy in marriage is doubtless true. But the fact that many are not happy is due to the fact that they are wrongfully united. It is a trite saying that oil and water will not mix and that Night is the opposite of Day. When the cold temperament unites with the warm, the simple with the saturnine, the shallow with the deep—can you wonder that there is uneasiness, misery and perhaps tragedy!

These facts were almost daily impressed upon my mind during the twenty-one years I practised Cheiromancy. Again and again in the consulting-room I heard confessions of secret unhappiness and emptiness of soul—not only from women but from men. Wives adrift! Husbands with their "secret consolations!" The reason was writ plain when I examined the hands stretched out to me, with the half-despairing cry that so often came to my ears: "Cheiro, I am so unhappy; what does the Future hold for me!"

This absence of pride in love sometimes brings with it the fatality that seals it as being the height of self-sacrifice. Not always is it on a woman's side, for I have recorded many instances of a man's self-sacrificing affection, that underlines the Scriptural saying: "For greater love hath no man than this: That a man lay down his life for his friend."

In this connection I draw from the archives of memory the case of Charles——, a highly educated man of promise, who for the sake of a love without pride "went out into the darkness," to make way for another. It is a story torn from the pages of Life, yet one that a novelist might construct.

I was in Paris during the year that the late Shah of Persia was in residence there, as a guest of the French Government. I have told elsewhere how I acquired great fame by first predicting the untimely death of King Humbert of Italy, and how three months later he was struck down by the hand of an assassin. This was copied into the Parisian papers, and as a result the Shah sent for me, and I achieved another remarkable success by telling him of events that were taking place in his far-distant capital of Teheran—facts that were confirmed by cable.

This brought a rush of clients to my rooms in Paris, and some very notable men and women came to see me.

One day a tall and highly-distinguished gentleman came in. He laid down a card, and as he did so, he said:

"Cheiro, I believe you can unravel the mysteries of human life, I believe, too, that you can lift the curtain that lies over the Future. My name must remain a sacred confidence with you. Tell me of myself, and the years yet unborn."

I cannot say more as to the identity of my visitor than that he was a French government official of the highest standing, distinguished as a poet and musician—a rare soul, because of his great gifts. Indeed, Nature seemed to have dowered him with a prodigal hand and the Cornucopia of talents seemed full to overflowing. Yet as I examined his sensitive hand I paused in doubt, for like the young man of Manoa, "there was one thing lacking"—a fatal, peace-shattering gap that I knew explained other ominous signs that were staring me in the face.

" You have great gifts and great opportunities. Fortune has smiled upon you."

He gave a mournful glance.

" All this is obvious, Cheiro. I do not want to know facts that are public property."

" But," I continued, without noticing the remark, " I find something wanting—and I fear that this ' something ' is the key to the melancholy and lassitude of soul that is destroying your peace of mind."

" Continue," he said tensely.

" You possess a wonderful capacity for faithful love. In your love is that rare quality—unselfishness! The affection that does indeed remain inviolate through all the vicissitudes of life, and even through disappointment and neglect."

A deep sigh, like a requiem for hopes that were perished, shook his frame. With a gesture, he encouraged me to continue.

" While you have success and worldly advantage," I went on, " you have no domestic happiness. Love is not returned. Nay, more, love is withheld."

He tore his hand away with a convulsive movement.

" Cheiro," he cried, " you are right—but would to God you were wrong. My wife is acclaimed as one of the loveliest women of the day—the most sprightly and talented, the theme of conversation in every select gathering. Yet a gulf divides us and I cannot pass it."

There was silence until he continued brokenly:

"But the Future—what of the Future? Will there be a change?"

As guardedly as I could I said that I believed a crisis was approaching; that self-control would be needed to meet it; that he ought to occupy his mind with his literary and musical pursuits.

After some conversation, he said quietly:

"Cheiro, I *understand.*" As he uttered these words a curious expression of self-exaltation, such as one imagines irradiated the faces of the martyrs of old, flitted across his face. With these words he passed from my sight.

After he had gone the train of my thoughts passed over his case. I knew his wife by repute, and I recalled that it was rumoured that she had a lover, for Parisian gossip leaves little to imagination. It was said that she was infatuated with her cousin—a debonair and dashing officer in a crack cavalry regiment. A presage of coming tragedy rested upon my mind.

Some months later, Paris was shocked by the news of the sudden death of Charles —— under circumstances that were rather mysterious. He was found dead in bed. Two bottles were on a table by the side of the bed—one containing a very harmless sedative that he was accustomed to take; the other, prussic acid. He had a hobby for chemical experiments so it was suggested that he needed the poison for some investigations he was making. The official explanation of his death was that, inadvertently, he had taken the poison instead of the draught, both bottles being almost exactly similar.

Soon afterwards the widow married the cousin!

I cannot recall a more striking example of the *fatal* and *selfless* love than that exhibited by Charles ——. It was there, signed upon his hand, and it was worked out in the fate of his life. When he realised that his wife had no love for him; when doubtless he discovered that her heart was given to her cousin—then he determined to stand aside and pass out into the night. Literally, he laid down his life for another.

I could relate many other instances that have come under my notice of similar devoted affections, that, unhappily, have not been sealed with the reciprocation that brings content.

CHAPTER IV

ABNORMAL HANDS

BETWEEN the steadfast lover, whose affection shines as tranquilly as the full moon, and the tempestuous lover, whose passion is like a headlong torrent sweeping away every obstacle, there will be found many curious divergents.

Most men and women are normal, or conform to type, in their affections, yet here and there may be met the abnormalities—individuals exhibiting the oddest and most disconcerting variations in their attitude towards the opposite sex.

Naturally, in my consulting room, where many secrets of the heart have been unveiled, I have listened to strange confessions from the lips of these people, or I have been able to tell them something of their peculiarities, and of the difficulties and even dangers that threatened them.

Zola, the great Realist who dissected human nature with the scapel of merciless introspection, said of Nana, whose love-affairs were legion: "Born under Saturn, this capricious creature really experienced a contempt for the opposite sex; she also played with them as a cat with a mouse—and the mousie invariably got the worst of it."

Few people probably realise the weight of this observation. Nana was an abnormality of the female species, but she was misjudged as being a Catherine or a La Ganeta—hungry for the love of men and ever avid for fresh experiences of human passion. In truth, she was devoid of passion, ever-cold and calculating—" born under Saturn."

I do not know whether Zola was a student of Cheiromancy, but if the rules of the Art had been applied to Nana's palm, I should expect to find her Line of Heart running from Saturn in *holes and links like a chain.* In man or woman, this significant marking denotes mental abnormality where love is concerned, and woe betide the person who is linked by Fate to such an individual.

When this line is pale and broad, without any depth, it denotes the *blasé* nature, without any depth of affection—the indifferent character, unable to warm with passion, or exhibit the mild sunshine of the affectionate disposition.

When set very low on the hand, almost touching the Line of Head, the heart will always interfere with the affairs of the head.

When it lies very high on the hand, and the space is narrowed only by the Head Line being abnormally high and out of its place, it indicates that the affairs of the heart are ruled by the head. Such persons are extremely calculating in affairs of love—the fortune hunter who marries for money, and who can subordinate passion for mercenary motives, will invariably be found to have this tell-tale line thus marked.

There is sometimes found in abnormal persons no Heart Line at all! It is a sign of the cold-blooded individual, who will stick at nothing to attain his end. Some of the most monstrous characters in the gallery of Crime are known to have been thus branded by Nature.

I can here interpose two striking instances that came under my personal notice.

While in my consulting rooms in London, I received a visit one day from a man of about fifty. He was handsome in a refined way, wore a full beard, and was dressed in irreproachable style. Yet I had an odd impression the moment he entered my room that I was in the presence of some Mystery of Iniquity. I examined his hands with uncommon interest.

His reason for visiting me was, he said, because he was engaged in speculations on the share market, and was "superstitious enough to believe that people had lucky and unlucky days." This was quite true, and I took pains to ascertain the days I thought would be favourable for him. I was proceeding to touch upon his personal characteristics, when he interrupted me brusquely.

"Cheiro, marriage and love and all that bosh does not interest me. If you can tell me how long I have to live—how much money I shall make—and whether I shall succeed in a new venture I am establishing—good! Otherwise, you are wasting my time and yours."

I made him acquainted with several facts concerning his commercial ventures and his length of days, and this seemed to satisfy him. But while I had been talking to him, I had, in a subconscious fashion, been observing his Line of Heart. It was ominous and significant! It told me plainly—and it was corroborated by his cold eyes, tight lips, and dominating habit of cynicism—that there was seated before me an abnormality. Indifferent to the opposite sex, yet he would be likely to pursue them for the purpose of inflicting cruelty upon them—mentally and, if possible, physically. That this was the hidden secret carried about by this handsome stranger, I could not doubt.

After some more conversation, he took his leave, having first signed my autograph book in a flourishing hand. The matter faded from my mind until some two years later, when I was dining with a friend, a prominent barrister, who remarked:

"Cheiro, I presume you come across many curious cases of men who are apparently dominated by evil?"

"Certainly," I replied.

"I suppose," he pursued, "that you attribute this to some singular planetary influence of a malignant character?"

The conversation developed on these lines, and was of a most interesting nature.

"I have asked you these questions, Cheiro," said my friend later, "because I must frankly confess that I am baffled by a case for which I have accepted a brief. A gentleman of the highest position, education, and I should imagine refinement, will be charged in a few hours with a series of crimes against women. The facts are so astounding that they will certainly create an unparalleled sensation. It appears that he has been in the habit of forming alliances with women under various names, courting them in a seemingly honourable fashion, leading them to repose confidence in him, and then—" The barrister paused, and I encouraged him to proceed. "It sounds impossible, I know," he pursued, "but having gained their confidence sufficiently to invite them to his chambers, he has then suddenly attacked them with a dog-whip, lashing them in a brutal fashion, and laughing in demoniac fashion while so doing. Three of the women thus assaulted held their tongues, fearing the disgrace of publicity; the fourth, a charming young girl of eighteen, revealed the facts to her parents, and they went at once to the police."

"Is this man well known?" I asked.

"As the facts will be made public in a few hours, there is no harm in telling you his name." The barrister mentioned it, and immediately a flood of light illuminated my mind. For the name he had told me was that of the gentleman who had declared his indifference to the opposite sex, and whose Line of Heart I had noted to be entirely absent.

"Why," I said slowly, "I know this man. He has visited my consulting room. He is entirely heartless—devoid of heart in the most complete sense."

My friend gazed at me in perplexity.

"Cheiro," he said, "you speak in riddles. But tell me what you can to explain this case, for I must confess that, with all my long experience of the Law, it baffles me."

Thereupon I explained that this man, devoid by nature of normal feelings and sympathy for the opposite sex, had in its place a contempt for women, allied with an overmastering desire to inflict pain upon them. He was an abnormality, a sex-monstrosity, and in fact was to be pitied. Only by patience and perseverance could he hope to overcome his terrible dominating passion, to inflict humiliation and suffering upon those women he selected under the guise of admiration.

The barrister remained silent for some time.

"Cheiro, your explanation has shed much light upon a difficult problem, but it does not help me; for the Law is no respecter of persons and cannot recognise any excuse save legal insanity. But you have filled me with pity for my client, where before I must confess I entertained feelings of disgust. I shall defend him with a determination to help him as much as I can."

The case created, as was expected, a great sensation. In the result the man was sentenced to two years' imprisonment, the Judge remarking that his conduct "was beyond excuse or extenuation." But if the learned occupant of the Bench had known as much of abnormalities as I did, and of this case in particular, he might have withheld these condemning words, and satisfied himself with pronouncing the sentence of the Law.

When I first went to America, I took a very fine apartment in the heart of Fifth Avenue, the most exclusive street in New York; with consulting-rooms in a famous hotel. But to make oneself known, without letters of introduction and without friends, is not a very easy matter.

My opportunity came, as already explained, when the *New York World* tested my powers, with a number of impressions of the hands of various people, whose names even I did not know.

It took the whole afternoon, from two o'clock until seven, before we had finished.

My very nervousness, I believe, made me succeed; my brain was screwed up to such a pitch that it seemed to drink in every line and formation, and made mental pictures of the subjects in such a way that I was able to describe their characteristics as if I had known them personally.

Then came the climax—it was about the fourth or fifth impression put before me.

"There is something in this hand so abnormal,"

I said, " that I shall refuse to read it unless you bring me the consent of the owner to tell what I see."

" We have the consent of all these people," was the reply, and I was shown a letter from the *New York World* stating that the consent had been obtained from the various persons who had given these impressions.

Under these conditions I agreed to proceed. The hand before me was that of a murderer, of that I was certain. I could make no mistake: on the left, all the lines were normal and showed a high degree of intelligence—but on the right the Heart Line was missing! There was such clear evidence that this man had used his intelligence to obtain money by crime, and that a little over the middle of his life his very self-confidence would betray him into the hands of the law.

" Whether this man has committed one murder or twenty," I remarked, " is not the question; at about his forty-fourth year, he will be tried for murder and condemned. It will be found that for years he has used his intelligence, and whatever profession he has followed, to obtain money by crime, and that he has stopped at nothing to obtain his ends. He will be condemned to the electric chair, will go under the greatest strain and anxiety, will live under the very shadow of death; but his life will not end in this manner, for he will pass the remainder of his life in prison."

The hand print was that of a Dr. Meyer who was convicted of insuring people's lives in Chicago—he was either their doctor, or managed later to attend them—and in exercising his profession it was believed that he poisoned his patients, and later collected the insurance money. At that time, in the States, one could insure any person, whether a relation or not, pay the premiums every year, and collect the money on the death of the individual. Since this affair occurred the law has been considerably altered.

When Dr. Meyer's case came on my prediction was fulfilled to the letter; after a long, sensational trial, in which he fought every inch of the ground, he was condemned to death, but within a few days of the date set for his execution the sentence was, on a technical point, altered to imprisonment for life.

When only one deep straight line is found running across the hand from side to side, the two Lines of Head and Heart appear to blend together. This denotes an intensely self-concentrated nature. Such persons, when they love, are as demons—every consideration, yes, and every obstacle must be swept aside. Women who have gone to the gallows for love are found in this class.

I would here interpose an interesting note made by a careful student of cheiromancy. The gentleman in question was a doctor, though it is unusual for a physician to be a student of the Lines on the

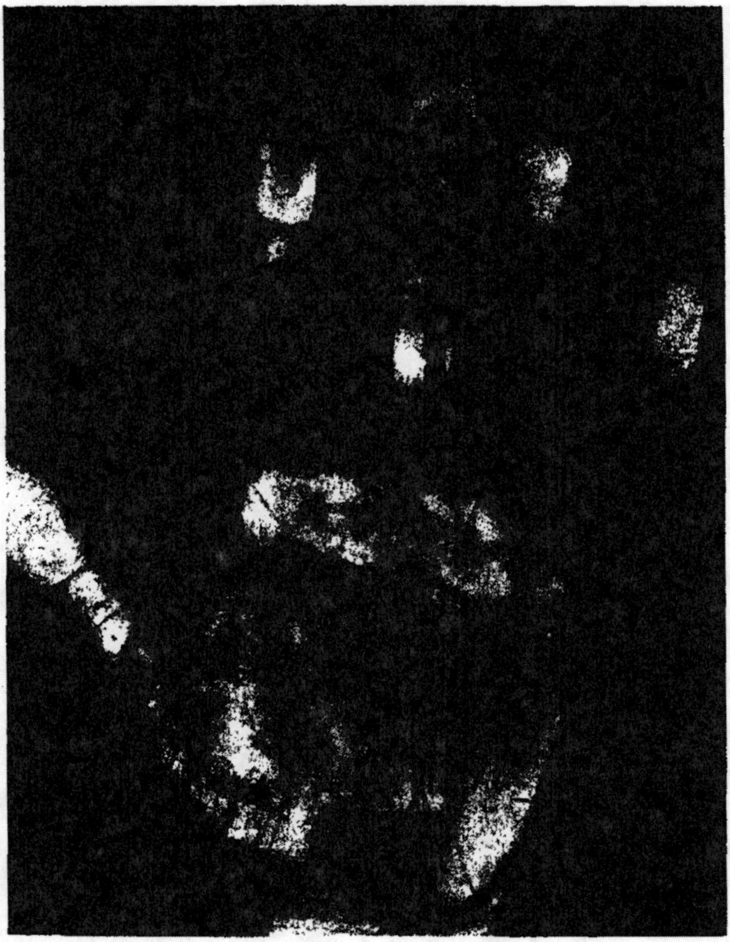

THE HAND OF A MURDERER

(DR. MEYER)

palm—a fact to be regretted, as much valuable information might thereby be obtained concerning the physical condition of the patient.

This doctor was one day called in to attend a young married woman in North London. As was his custom, he noted the lines on her hand, and he was struck particularly with the blending of Head and Heart Lines in one straight, strong furrow. At the time, the woman was apparently happily married to a good husband, yet suddenly the whole of the country was startled by a fearful tragedy, in which this woman figured as the chief character.

She was madly in love with another man—a man who was married and who lived happily with his wife and one child. In a weak moment he pandered to the passion of the woman—and thereby added a hundredfold to the blaze of destroying love that was resolved, *at all cost*, to attain its objective.

This objective meant that she must be the wife of the man whom she loved. Therefore Murder alone could bring about the attainment of her desires, for two lives stood in the way.

She determined to rid herself first of the wife of her lover. Cunningly inviting the woman to tea in her house in Hampstead, there ensued a scene that beggared fiction. While the innocent woman was at the tea-table she was suddenly struck down by a butcher's cleaver wielded by the love-maddened hostess. The visitor had brought her infant with her, and it woke up with a wailing cry. It was also despatched with a blow of the cleaver.

The shades of evening were falling when the murderess wheeled through the streets a perambulator, upon which was a huge bundle wrapped in oilcloth. It was the body of her victim and the little babe. When darkness fell, she met the unsuspecting husband of the murdered woman, kissed him fondly, and made use of this expression :

" I have a feeling, dearest, that soon we shall always be together."

Later he parted from her, and sought his home. It was in darkness !

This is no fanciful narrative, for the murderess was Mrs. Pearcey, who paid the penalty upon the scaffold for the murder of Mrs. Hogg and her infant child. In all records of criminology, it is doubtful if there can be found a more demoniac lover than Mrs. Pearcey, who did not hesitate to stoop to murder in order to accomplish her insane desire to " possess entirely her wonderful lover."

CHAPTER V

THE LINE OF MARRIAGE

CERTAIN marks on the Mount of Mercury relate to marriage, although the word " marriage " really means the mating or coming together of two individuals, and not the mere words of a ceremony that often is meaningless.

The truth is that these lines seen under the little fingers merely register the influence of different people over our lives—what kind of influence they have had, the effect produced, and all that is in accordance with such influence.

Now, marriage being so important an event in one's life, it follows that, if events can be foretold by the hand, marriage should certainly be marked thereon, even years in advance. I have always found that such is the case in respect to all important influences; it is also natural that *affaires de cœur*, liasons, and so forth, can be thus singled out and divided from what is known as marriage, except when the liason is just as important and the influence on the life just as strong.

Why there should be a time set apart in our life to marry, or not to marry as the case may be, can only be answered by referring to the other mysteries that surround us.

If any one can explain why a magnet brought into a room has the power to magnetise every other bit of iron in the room, what the power is, and what the connection, then he may be able to answer the other question; but until all the secret laws and forces of Nature are known, we can take no other standpoint than to accept those strange anomalies, without having the power to answer the cry of the curious — the perpetual, parrot-like "Why?" of the doubting.

The only theory I advance is that, as the press of the finger on the keyboard in New York at the same moment affects the keyboard in London, so by the medium of the ether, which is more subtle than electricity, all persons are consciously or unconsciously in touch with, and in communion with one another.

The true Line of Marriage is found between the end of the Line of Heart and the base of the fourth finger.

This perhaps is an opportune moment to reveal that even Queen Mary, well ballasted as she is by common sense, does not disdain belief in palmistry. On the occasion of her wedding, I ventured to send her a copy of my exhaustive work on palmistry, and from the hand of Madame Bricks, at that time her confidential lady-in-waiting, I received a personal letter from the Princess May, as she was then known. In this letter, dated from White Lodge, Richmond—where she resided with the Duchess of Teck prior to her marriage—she expressed her pleasure at the gift, and stated that it would be among the "most prized of her wedding-gifts."

It was in fact whispered in Society—and I can neither deny nor confirm it—that when the young Princess was betrothed to the ill-fated Duke of Clarence, she had called in company with a lady-in-waiting at my consulting rooms in Bond Street, concealing her identity for the best of reasons. It was reported that I had said emphatically that her betrothal would end in the sorrow of bereavement; that it would be succeeded by another engagement

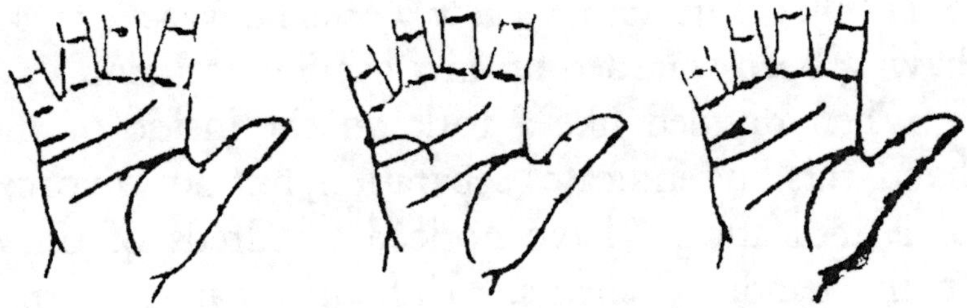

FIG 6. FIG 7. FIG 8.

THE LINE OF MARRIAGE

to a brother; and that the highest honours and felicity would succeed in after days. It was some weeks later that the young Duke died at Sandringham; the rest is history.

In Fig. 6 will be found a representation of a straight and clear line that indicates a happy union.

Persons with such a line upon their palm draw a lucky number in the Lottery of Hearts and are to be congratulated upon their good fortune.

When the line curves downwards towards the palm, as in Fig. 7, it indicates the death of the marriage partner. Again and again in my consulting room I have seen this significant mark, and have drawn my own conclusions; for there are times when, for pity's sake, I have felt it necessary to use reticence in order to avoid inflicting needless sorrow.

I recall a young man calling upon me with such a line in his hand. Poor fellow! He was in the hey-dey of honeymoon happiness, and I had not the heart to point out the ominous fate that hovered over him. But within a few weeks he was a corpse, having been smashed up in a cycling accident.

When divided like a fork on the inside of the hand, this line indicates separation, but not divorce. This indication I have noticed hundreds of times in the hands of clients. Unhappy marriages that are ended for all practical purposes by separation, but for various reasons are not terminated by the Law, are shown by this sign. See Fig. 8.

When this fork-like appearance is shown on the outside, difficulties, delays, and separation will occur before marriage.

A lady called upon me one day and showed me her hand for a reading. She was not young; probably nearing forty, although well preserved. I found this indication very strongly marked, and I did not hesitate to give my opinion.

" You have had a deep love disappointment in your life, and it persists even now."

She sighed as she answered.

" True, Cheiro, but I think I have now reconciled myself to it."

" The time is coming, and very shortly, when your mourning will be turned into gladness, and in the most unexpected fashion."

" I fear that will never be," she returned. "My lover left me nearly fifteen years ago. It was a misunderstanding—a stupid affair, but Pride barred the path to reconciliation, and he went off to the Antipodes. I have never ceased to want him and long for his return. But not one single word have I heard from that day to this. Of course, by this time he must be married, and will long ago have forgotten about me."

I think it was about six months later that she visited me again. She seemed like another woman, and radiated gaiety and happiness. With her was a fine-looking man of about forty-five, who was introduced as her husband. A romantic story followed.

A short time after she had left my consulting room she had met her long-lost lover walking down the Strand. There had been an instant recognition. He had made a fortune " down under," and was in England for six months holiday. He had been longing to write many times, but had said, "Of course, she will be married by now." When he found that she was still unwed, he took out a special license there and then.

These marks may seem trifles to the inexperienced, but in twenty-one years experience I have never found them to go astray. It is curious that most of the really happy marriages are prefaced by difficulties and delays—hence, I suppose, the old

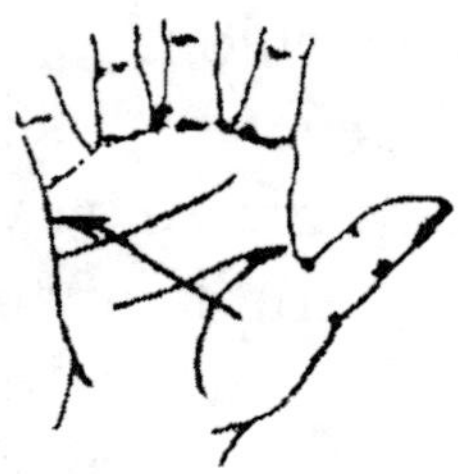

FIG 9. THE LINE OF MARRIAGE

saying that the course of true love never did run smooth!

The indications of divorce upon the hand are clear, and cannot be disregarded in reading a hand.

When the Line of Marriage curves downwards in a fork, with a line crossing to the ball of the thumb, divorce is indicated to the person on whose hand this mark appears. See Fig. 9.

I recollect that I was, on one occasion, at the house of a lady who led fashion during the Edwardian period. A very select company indeed was gathered at dinner, and the conversation turned upon the occult.

"Be careful," said my hostess archly, to a male guest who was hotly declaiming that palmistry was "all a fraud." "We have a very distinguished Seer with us this evening!" She pointed to myself, and I was inclined to blush before the curious glances bent upon me.

But this particular guest could not let the subject alone. After dinner, in the drawing-room, he brought it up again.

"I will stake my reputation that nobody could tell me anything about my Past or Future."

With this, he darted a very meaning look in my direction. I was never loath to accept a challenge.

"I make no vain boasts, but if you will allow me to examine your palm, perhaps I can tell you something. I do so on condition that you acknowledge whether I am right or wrong."

The other guests gathered round to enjoy the joke. As I examined the palms held out to me, I saw at once the word "Divorce" writ large, and I saw too that it had taken place some time before. Now, this guest had always boasted himself a heart-whole bachelor—"I have never yet found the woman who could make me bow my will to hers," he often boasted.

I told him a few general things, which he acknowledged were true. Then, fixing my eyes full on his confident face, I said:

"Now I come to your divorce."

He started and half drew away his hand.

"You are joking, Cheiro," he said feebly, but his face grew pale.

"Your divorce," I proceeded firmly, "which took place some eight years ago. If you wish, I will detail some of the circumstances, but it was a singularly painful affair. Your wife's lover——"

He stopped me with a gesture of infinite pain and disgust.

"Enough, Cheiro, I have wronged you!"

Without another word, beyond a muttered "Good night" to the hostess, he slunk out of the room. As may be imagined, the affair created considerable gossip and various versions of the affair appeared in the gossip paragraphs of the newspapers.

When the Line of Marriage cuts downwards through the Line of Success, the subject will lose position and riches by marriage.

The Line of Marriage ending in a fork, with a line from it joining the Line of Heart, and the latter curving downwards, indicates a very unhappy marriage—due to the exacting nature of the person upon whose hand the sign appears. In this case, there may never be separation or divorce, but it threatens a violent end to the marriage—death by violence is usually the verdict of the jury. These two lines are illustrated in Fig. 10 and Fig. 11.

While I was in America I was asked to read the hands of a "very loving couple," who called upon me and said that they had recently been married. But in the hand of the lady was this sinister sign ; I looked with apprehension and compassion upon the weak face of the bridegroom, and wondered what the months had in store for him. They both signed their names in my autograph book, and as they left, the lady had the final word.

" Oh, thank you so much, Cheiro, for your wonderful talk. I am sure both myself and my husband will never forget it."

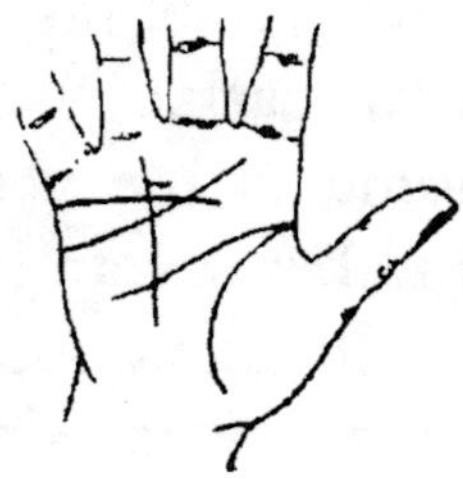

FIG 10.

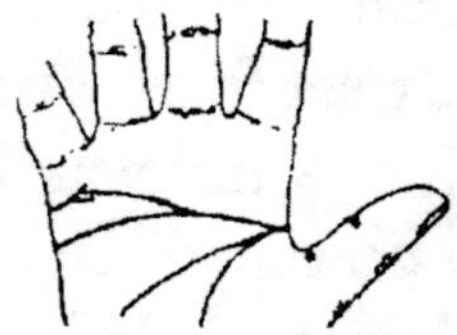

FIG 11.

THE LINE OF MARRIAGE

I was on the point of leaving America, some time later, after having traversed the whole of the United States, when my eye caught a sensational news story. It related that, in Washington, a woman had been arrested for poisoning her husband, the motive alleged being her desire to obtain his insurance money. It was the " affectionate wife " and it appeared from the evidence at the trial—where she was found guilty and sent to penal servitude for life—that she had poisoned the poor fellow with arsenic, while apparently treating him with wifely tenderness. Nature's signs are there for those who can read them. Unhappily, too often they cannot be read, or the warning goes unheeded.

The Line of Marriage, with a line from it running into the Line of Head, indicates that unhappiness and disputes will be caused by the opposition of the mental views of the parties. Particularly does this show religious differences, and I have noted scores of cases where Protestants and Roman Catholics have had their differences over the bringing up of the children—this bickering being plainly set forth by this particular mark.

This point was brought home to me very forcibly on one occasion, when a rather severe-looking gentleman called upon me. He mentioned that he was about to be married to a lady considerably his junior, and I gathered from his conversation that he was somewhat diffident as to how the match would turn out. He was particularly pressing to be told whether this disparity of age would make any difference to his happiness.

After I had examined his hand, I noticed very distinctly the mark I have described above; indeed, in all my experiences, I do not think I have ever seen a plainer indication of future trouble from religious differences.

" If you desire me to tell you everything, will you inform me if you are an ardent Roman Catholic?"

He looked surprised.

"Yes, Cheiro, I am, and all my family have been for generations."

"In that case, I fear I must tell you that your coming marriage will not turn out happily."

A pained look crossed his face.

"Is it because of our disparity in age—or is there another man who stands in my path?" he asked.

"Age has nothing to do with it," I replied. "Indeed, in many ways, it will prove an ideal marriage. There is certainly no rival in your path, but you are a man of invincible religious conviction. Nothing will shake you in that direction. But I also foresee almost similar obstinacy in another direction. The lady who is to be your wife will dispute with you as to how your firstborn child is to be brought up—in what faith, Roman Catholic or Protestant. That will be the rock upon which the happiness of your union will be shattered."

A relieved expression lightened his features.

"Cheiro," he said, "you are wrong. I do not dispute that you have skill in certain phases of the occult, and in reading the hand. But in what you have just said, you are entirely deceived. The lady has pledged her word to me that if there should be any children of our marriage, they shall be brought up as Roman Catholics. It is true that she is a Protestant—that one fact alone dims my happiness. But she is, so to speak, a lukewarm Protestant, and

I have earnest hopes that she may be converted to the Ancient Faith."

With the utterance of these words, the light of the fanatic crossed his pale features.

He signed my book and departed.

I afterwards visited Paris and America, came back to London, and was once again in my old rooms. I suppose nearly seven years had passed, when one afternoon this gentleman entered my consulting-room. But I saw in a moment that the passage of Time had not rested lightly upon him. His hair was powdered with white; his chiselled features were sterner; his lips more compressed.

He seated himself, and a sigh seemed to rend his breast.

"Cheiro," he said at length, "I have not come here to-day for any other purpose than to testify to the remarkable power of your Art. All that you predicted has come to pass. My wife and I are on the verge of separation—perhaps legal proceedings. I recall your prophetic words, 'the rock upon which the happiness of your union will be shattered will be religious differences.' The first months of our marriage proved an idyll. Madeline was as charming as an opening flower, blossoming into greater perfection. She entered into my pursuits, she was the life and soul of the house, and our love consecrated the hours. Then came the birth of our little son. In the ardour of my joy, I did not notice the tardiness of her recovery, or perceive that a deep melancholy was settling upon her spirits. There followed a restoration to indifferent health. She was changed—mysteriously changed, nor could I penetrate the secret of the estrangement.

"There came a period of religious depression, bordering upon mania. She became obsessed with the idea that she had committed some unpardonable sin. Instead of laxness, as before, in her attendance at her Church, she became almost a slave to it. Morning, noon, and night—wet or fine—she presented herself at her Church. The Vicar became her closest friend—her spiritual guide and comforter. The climax came when one day she informed me that her little son must be brought up in the Protestant faith. I resisted; scenes followed. I was surprised, almost terrified, by her obstinacy and tenacity. Yet . . . what could I do. My faith was as dear as hers. In this seething controversy, love perished and died; we wrangled over the soul of our little son, while the priests looked on complacently—for naturally my spiritual advisers said that I was right, while her vicar was sure that she was right. Now, Cheiro, the end has come. We must part. The law is to be invoked—the law which will scatter the dying embers of the fire that once warmed our hearts."

I leave this story without comment.

It is a melancholy fact that religious differences have sundered many marriages that might otherwise have proved most happy. Whenever I see the fatal mark of religious controversy, I have always endeavoured to *warn* my clients of the possibilities. If there is a broad-minded effort on both sides to avoid disputes that end in bitterness, then the danger may be passed: for it cannot be too strongly impressed upon my readers that these marks carry their message of warning, so that much trouble and disaster may be avoided by taking prompt action before it is too late.

CHAPTER VI

CURIOUS MARRIAGE SIGNS

So remarkable are the variations of the lines, islands, loops, and so on, connected with the Line of Marriage, that almost a volume might be written on this most intriguing sign. During the whole of my twenty-one years of actual practice of the science of Cheiromancy, I was always learning something fresh and turning this knowledge to practical account. For it must not be forgotten that the lines on any two persons' hands are never exactly similar.

When the Line of Marriage forms into an island and has a strong drooping curve, some protracted sorrow, such as an illness or severe misfortune, will end the life of the partner to the marriage. It is an infallible guide to misfortune, to husband or wife as the case may be. See Fig. 12.

While I was in Paris, I had a poignant example of this in my own experience.

A very fine-looking young woman called upon me; a Countess in her own right, whose father was prominent in the De Lesseps Panama investigations. She told me that she had just been married to a man who was passionately in love with her, the passion was returned. It was, in fact, an ideal match—yet there hung over her an indefinable sense of gloom and a premonition of coming evil. Without saying anything to her husband, who himself was radiantly happy, she had come to consult me, having heard of my fame through a mutual friend.

I examined her delicate hand, and there I saw, in unmistakable clearness, the fatal sign that her partner in matrimony would be cut off by a violent

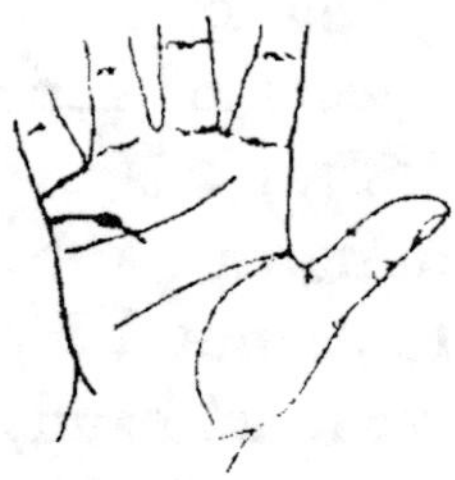

FIG 12. THE LINE OF MARRIAGE

death. As I saw evidence that the event would not be long delayed, I debated whether I should say anything concerning it. At last I told her, as gently as possible, that sometimes a premonition was sent as a *warning*; I gathered that her husband was a headlong impulsive fellow, very fond of fast motoring and dangerous sports. It would be as well if he used the utmost caution. She thanked me and went away.

I do not know if she conveyed my warning to her husband, but some four months later he met his death, while motoring at a terrific speed between

Paris and Melun, being killed instantly. I was only able to warn; more I could not do.

I have told elsewhere how I warned Mr. Stead concerning journeys by water, having predicted his death by drowning some years before the sinking of the ill-fated "Titanic," whereby he lost his life. He himself had a strange conviction that he would be killed by a mob in the streets of London; nothing I could say would shake this impression. But though I *warned* him, it did not prevent him from

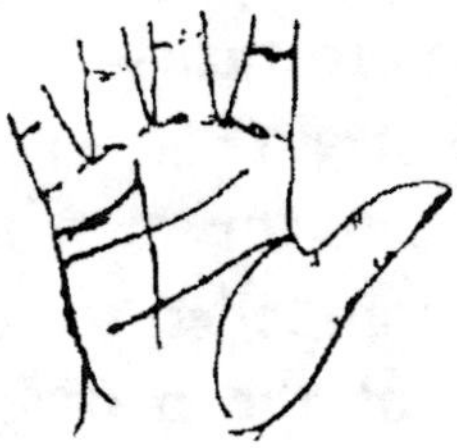

FIG 13.

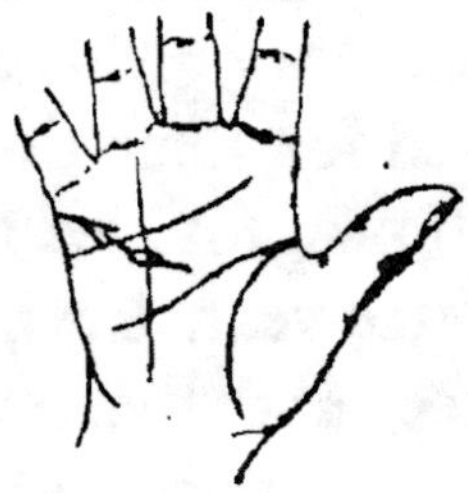

FIG 14.

THE LINE OF MARRIAGE

making the journey. I have sometimes thought that as he stood upon the sinking ship, my words must have flashed into his mind: "I foresee death by drowning—there is danger in the House of Water."

Reverting to the Line of Marriage, if a fine line is seen passing from it upwards into the Line of Success, under the third finger, marriage will bring success and wealth. See Fig. 13.

An ominous sign, and one that I always disliked to encounter, is when the Line of Marriage terminates in a fork, with a line from it forming an island on the Line of Success, for the union will end in scandal, loss of position, and disgrace. See Fig. 14.

I remember a gentleman consulting me immediately before his marriage. I must not reveal his name, as his father is still a revered head of a vast business enterprise. But I saw immediately that the match would end in disaster, and as plainly as I could I said so. When I had finished speaking, the prospective bridegroom burst out laughing.

"Well, Cheiro, I think you are an amusing old fraud. My marriage is going to be the finest there ever was. My girl is a topping creature—" and he continued for some time in this strain.

But time provides the acid test for matrimony. Some three years later, he was compelled to sue for a divorce, and the revelations of the married life of the pair were sensational. She had been, it appears, a barmaid, and soon after marriage both gave way to drink. Wretchedness was piled upon wretchedness, until she eloped with a notorious man about Town, when the marriage was dissolved amid a cloud of scandal.

There are two highly significant lines connected with marriage with which I shall now deal. I append a plate of them.

Fig. 15 illustrates the Lines of Marriage, starting with an island. I have always regarded this as an ominous sign, indicative of seduction and trouble before marriage. But if the line continues straight and clear, all will come right in the end. I have had remarkable confirmation of this in my consulting-room experience, but naturally in matters of such delicacy, a seal of secrecy must be preserved.

When the Line of Marriage is very short, and curves upwards at the end (see Fig. 16), marriage is not likely to take place at any time. I have often been asked by women if they will ever be married, and when sometimes I have been compelled to give a negative reply, they were usually incredulous. But I can honestly record that during twenty-one

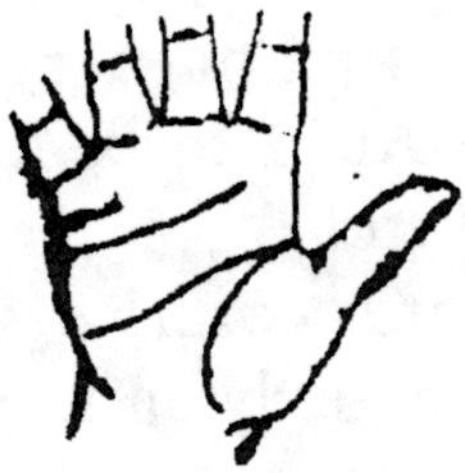

FIG 15.

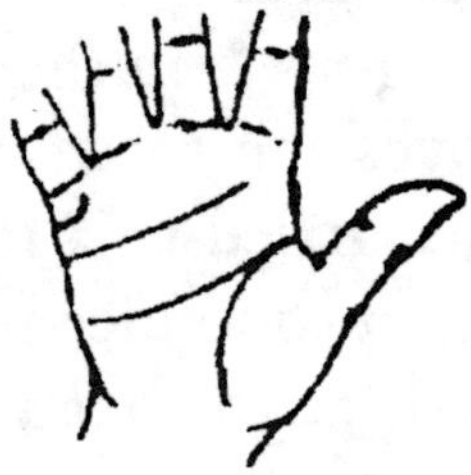

FIG 16.

THE LINE OF MARRIAGE

years experience of my Art, I have never known this sign to err.

Sometimes the realisation of this prediction has been accomplished by dramatic developments.

In my early career in London, I was consulted by a dashing young lady, who was very well known in Society as being one of the leaders of the smart set. She was engaged to a man who was quite a figure in the gay world—a Russian Count, whose clothes, parties, and bachelor establishment were very freely paragraphed.

There was no question that the lady was madly

in love with the debonair Count. One night she was at a party when my Art was discussed, and she determined to pay me a visit—for she was endowed with all the curiosity of her sex, and was most anxious to know what the Future held for her.

I told her a good many incidents connected with her past life, and these she owned were quite correct. But what I knew rested upon her mind was to hear something of her Future.

"Tell me, Cheiro," she asked abruptly, "will my marriage turn out well? You know I'm frightfully 'gone' on the man to whom I'm engaged and he loves me to desperation. Am I to be a happy wife, married to a model husband?"

She pronounced these words with a slightly cynical laugh, but I felt that, underlying it, was an acute anxiety.

What could I tell her? Graved on the shapely palm was the mark I have just described, that told the fatal news that she was not destined to be a wife. Moreover I discerned that the reason was connected with the man and that his career was about to terminate in a cloud of scandal and disgrace.

As gently as I could, I hinted that I feared a disappointment was in store for her. When she grasped its import, she spoke angrily.

"Cheiro, this is absurd! Why, there cannot be found a more devoted lover than my man, while for my part I would go through fire and water to marry him. I'm sorry I came here, for I do not believe you." With this she left me, in some anger.

Some months later, I was dining at a famous restaurant with a small party, when one of the male guests remarked:

"Have you heard the sensational news about the Count?" He mentioned the name of the Russian. We all said that we had heard nothing.

"He has been arrested for an attempted swindle upon a City merchant. It is alleged that he is an impostor, and is 'wanted' all over the Continent for frauds."

This was indeed a sensational piece of news, and it proved true. The "Count" was no Count at all, but a masquerader who preyed upon the wealthy. He was tried, but through some technical flaw in the indictment, he got off. He was ordered to be deported, and was sent back to Russia.

The lady was struck to the heart by this revelation of his criminal life. Her grief was such that she turned to religion for consolation, and being a Roman Catholic, she decided to take the veil. She is now immured in a nunnery, so marriage is out of the question. What to her had seemed impossible, was registered upon her hand, and in the slow workings of Fate came to be a reality.

Some interesting facts concerning Marriage are shown by the "Influence Lines" joining the Line of Fate. By the changes in the appearance of the latter, after the junction with the line, the result or effect of the union or marriage may be deduced.

If the Line of Fate appears stronger from the date where the "Influence Line" joins it, the marriage will have brought success. If fainter or broken up in islands or pieces, then the marriage has brought failure and ill-luck.

The number of children of a marriage is a very interesting subject, and this is fully set forth upon the hand. Incredible as it must seem to the novice, by a deep study of the fine lines that rise upwards from the Line of Marriage, it will be found that decided or strong lines indicate boys; fine lines, girls. I always found it useful to employ a magnifying glass in examining these lines, for sometimes they are so faint as to be almost invisible to the naked eye. In time, great accuracy can be attained in determining the size and composition of a client's family.

A very good plan, in trying to see these lines, is to press this portion of the hand with the tips of the fingers, and then note which of these small lines stand out the most clearly.

Sometimes they are extremely deeply marked, and as a rule much more so on a woman's hand than on a man's.

When they appear as straight lines, they denote strong healthy children, but when very faint or crooked, the children indicated are always delicate.

When the first part of the little line (taking it

upward from the Line of Marriage) is marked with a small "island," such a child will be very delicate in its early life, but if the line appears well marked when the "island" is passed, the probability is that it will grow up strong and healthy. When ending or broken at the "island," the child will not grow up.

When one line stands out very clear and distinct among the others, the child indicated by the mark will be more to the parent, and will be more successful than any of the others.

To know the number of children anyone will have, it is necessary to count these lines from the outside of the hand in toward the palm.

The Bracelet is represented by the line or lines at the wrist, or extreme base of the palm—we do not pay much attention to these lines nowadays, as we can learn all we need know from the palm itself. But when the uppermost of the Bracelet Lines arches upwards into the palm, it appears to be a very reliable sign of sterility—particularly when seen on a woman's hand.

Some further important hints concerning marriage will be found in the following notes :

When the Line of Marriage on the Mount of Mercury is distinct, but with fine hair lines dropping from it, it denotes trouble brought on by illness on the opposite side. I have proved this innumerable times by close observation.

When the end of the line droops, or curves downwards towards the Line of Heart, it tells that the person with whom the subject is connected will die first. When the line curves upwards, the possessor is not likely to marry again.

When the line has an island in the centre, or at any portion, it foretells some very heavy trouble in the married life—a separation of some kind, but not by law.

When there is a short line running parallel, and almost touching the marriage line, it tells of some

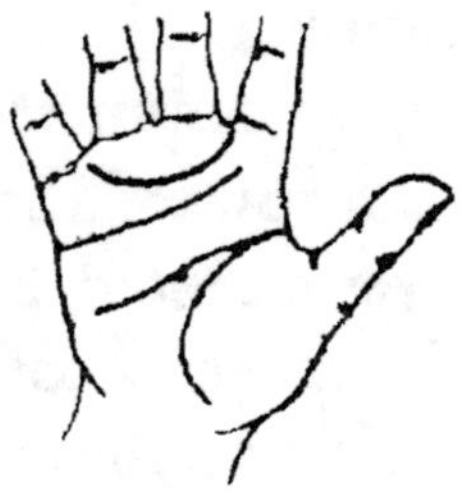

FIG 17. THE GIRDLE OF VENUS

deep affection, after marriage, on the side of the person on whose hand it appears.

The study of these marks relating to Marriage is a most fascinating pursuit. There is still much to be learned, and even after years of the most minute examinations, I am always ready to learn something new concerning the marks that point to Fate—and Marriage.

Some very interesting observations may be made concerning the Girdle of Venus and its relation to love and marriage.

The Girdle is generally found as a kind of semicircle, rising between the first and second fingers, and ending between the third and fourth. See Fig. 17.

I have not in my experience found this mark to indicate the gross sensuality that is so often ascribed to it by other writers. It should be remembered that the hand is divided by the Line of Head, as it were, into two hemispheres, the lower and the upper.

The lower relates to the physical or more animal side of the nature, and the upper to the intellectual. Following this arrangement, it is only reasonable to assume that this mark under consideration, viz., the Girdle of Venus, relates more to the mental side of the symbolism of the Venus nature.

I have found that persons with this sign are more mentally sensual than physically so. They love to read or write books on the subject of the "sex problem," but they are not inclined to put their theories and ideas into practice, at least with their own lives.

The qualities, however, that this mark represents are much more active and dangerous when this Girdle forms itself from the Mount of Saturn to that of Mercury. The imaginings of such people are then morbid and unhealthy.

To those who study Astrology, the inference that I draw from the connection of these two parts of the hand will become clear and reasonable.

When broken or made up of little pieces, the

Girdle of Venus has little meaning—except to show an hysterical temperament, with a leaning towards the tendencies I have mentioned above.

These persons suffer enormously from moods, they are very difficult to live with, and when the Girdle of Venus runs off the side of the hand and passes out through the Marriage Lines, their moody, changeable natures generally make marriage for them an unusually unhappy experience.

PART II

LIFE AND DEATH

CHAPTER VII

THE LINE OF LIFE EXPLAINED

"*What we know as Life is but existence;*
A waiting-place, a haven by the sea—
A little space amid unmeasured distance,
A glimpse, a vista, of that life to be."

CHEIRO.

"SHOW me my days and the measure of my life what it is: and behold, I will walk softly in the shadow of this knowledge."

Thus wrote the Psalmist David, nor is it difficult to catch the meaning of the sweet singer of Israel.

He desired to know something of the allotted portion of his years, that he might use Time with economy, and be found ready to carry out Life's duties in the full knowledge that this existence was but a prelude to a wider and a better one.

When considering the Line of Life—one of the most important lines upon the palm of the hand—I desire to make it clear that such an examination is not undertaken solely to afford any person some idea of a long or a short life.

I want to correct some misconceptions.

To begin with, the great majority of individuals

labour under the impression that a long Line of Life, going round the base of the Mount of Venus, indicates a long existence. It may do; on the other hand, there are so many other indications and considerations to weigh in the balance, that it is just as likely that the days of the years may not be protracted beyond middle-age, or even less.

I would rather say that, if the line is perfect—without serious breaks, crosses, or irregularities of any kind—it does promise that life should be healthy and reasonably long. But how rarely is the line thus found. It is of the greatest importance in considering the Line of Life, to examine and to understand the Line of Health—a sort of subsidiary line, and one that is too often overlooked by those professors of Cheiromancy who have not made a deep and prolonged study of the art of reading the lines of the hand.

The Line of Life is that line which runs round the base of the thumb and lies directly over a large blood-vessel called the great Palmer Arch (see Map of the Hand). This blood-vessel is closely connected with the heart, stomach and vital organs, a fact which may have given rise to its name "The Vital," as used by the ancients.

It is reasonable to assume that it is this intimate connection with the vital organs of the body which enables it to foretell the probable length of life judged solely from natural causes.

If the student will bear this in mind, it will make

clear and plain to him many difficulties in connection with predictions as to health and disease, and he will follow more easily the following explanations.

The first rule to master is that, to be normal, the Line of Life should be long, clearly marked, and without any irregularities or breaks of any kind. Such a formation would indicate vitality, freedom from illness, and strength of constitution.

As the Line of Life represents the stomach and the vital organs, when well marked the stomach and digestion must necessarily be in a good condition.

When made up of little pieces or linked like a chain, it is a certain sign of poor health, weak stomach and lack of vitality.

As the Line of Life seems in every sense to be the representative on the hand of the body or trunk of the subject—so the position of these breaks, marks, links or islands denotes the portion of the body most affected.

Before we go farther, I must also impress on the student to grasp the fact that every line or sign on the hand plays a dual role. By one of their roles these lines indicate the disease to which the person is most liable for the entire run of the life, and in another role these lines indicate the date when the illness will reach its greatest gravity.

To explain carefully this strange phenomenon of nature, I have divided this line into sections (see

Special Plate), and although I am not writing on astrology in these pages, yet all believers in that science may be interested to find how wonderfully these twin sciences agree, when the comparison is pointed out by an impartial observer, such as I claim to be.

In the Special Plate are shown the Sections of the Line of Life with their various tendencies, divided by the mounts at the base of the fingers. This will

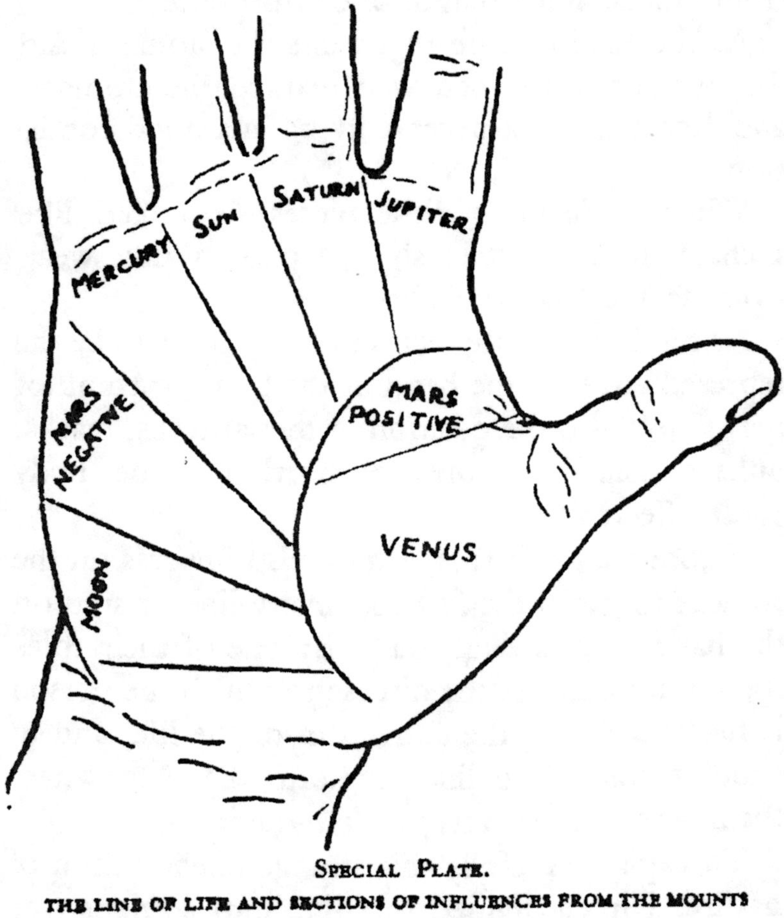

SPECIAL PLATE.

THE LINE OF LIFE AND SECTIONS OF INFLUENCES FROM THE MOUNTS

materially assist the student to comprehend their significance, and will enable him to obtain an accuracy on all matters relating to health, diseases, and dangers to the life, that up till now has never been attained.

We will now proceed to consider the details as regards the Line of Life itself.

The Line of Life rises under the Mount of Jupiter and running down the hand, encircles the Mount of Venus.

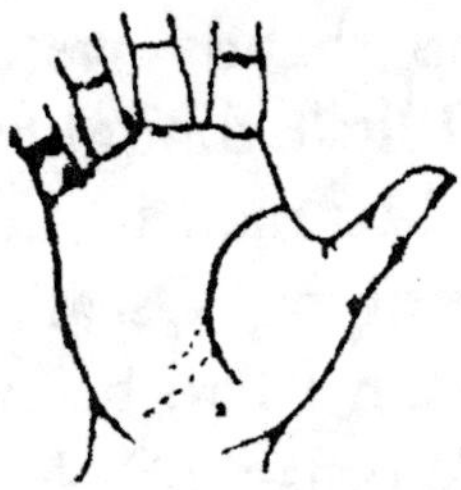

FIG 18.

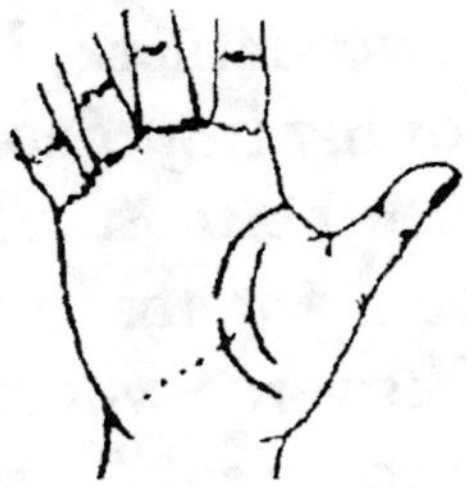

FIG 19.

THE LINE OF LIFE

Lines passing from the Line of Life towards the opposite side of the palm promise long travels and voyages, as indicated by the dotted lines in Fig. 18. But if the main line continues deeply marked round the ball of the thumb, the person will always return to their own country. If the Life Line is broken, as in Fig. 19, it indicates a very severe illness, or if seen in both hands, then death. If however a sister line is seen guarding the break as in Fig. 19, it promises recovery no matter how serious the illness may be.

On the other hand, if the Line of Life bends

outwards towards the opposite side of the palm, that person will end their days in a far-off land.

One of the most striking illustrations of this that ever came under my notice was in connection with Oscar Wilde.

In the earlier days of my career, I was called to the house of a famous society hostess, who was entertaining a large number of celebrities. I was required to read various hands that were passed through a red velvet curtain—the idea being that I should not know whose hands I was reading.

When two rather plump hands were passed through for my inspection, I little thought that they belonged to the most talked-of man in London at that period; for that very night, Oscar Wilde (I learned afterwards whose palm I had been examining) had produced "The Woman of No Importance," one of his greatest plays. I was however so struck with the difference in the markings between the left and the right hands that I explained that the left denoted the hereditary tendencies, while the right showed the developed or attained characteristics; when we use the left side of the brain the nerves cross and go to the right hand. So that the right shows the true nature and development of the individual.

I pointed out the marks on Oscar Wilde's hands as an example where the left had promised the most unusual brilliancy and uninterrupted success, which was completely broken and ruined at a certain

date in the right. Almost forgetting myself for a moment, I summed up by saying: "The left hand is the hand of a king, but the right hand that of a king who will send himself into exile, and die in a strange land, alone and friendless."

At this, there was a shout of ironical laughter from the company, who knew that I had been reading the hands of the most successful man in England.

But the owner of the hands did not laugh.

"At what date?" he asked quietly.

"A few years from now will come exile," I replied. "I should say between your forty-first and forty-second year. The end of life will follow a few years later."

Wilde came out from behind the curtain, and was greeted with uproarious laughter by the company, who thought it an excellent joke.

The great dramatist turned to them gravely, and repeated in his wonderful voice:

"The left is the hand of a king, but the right is that of a king who will send himself into exile."

With that, he left the room without another word.

I did not meet Oscar Wilde again until shortly before he commenced the action against the Marquis of Queensbery that was to end so fatally for his reputation. He came and asked me if the break was still there? I told him that it was. In a far-off voice he said: "My good friend, if my Destiny

Missing Page

Page No. 108

This page is missing in the source file, if you find this page in future, please share with us at books@gyanbooks.com for the betterment of future readers and the society.

Missing Page

Page No. 109

This page is missing in the source file, if you find this page in future, please share with us at books@gyanbooks.com for the betterment of future readers and the society.

Russia, I had been called to the Winter Palace, and had there discussed deep matters of Fate and Life and Death with the Emperor of that great country. It was, doubtless, owing to the fame gained by these momentous interviews, the accounts of which got into the public press, that I was invited while in Rome to see King Humbert of Italy.

I found His Majesty remarkably unassuming and business-like in manner. He had already been the victim of an attempted assassination, and it had left its mark upon him. But Humbert was a brave man and although he knew, despite the efforts of his secret police, that enemies swarmed around him, he would not give up any of his work. In his unassuming way he continued to visit various parts of his Kingdom, and showed himself to the people in an absolutely fearless fashion.

After some preliminary conversation, I examined his hand. I must admit that I was startled to see that his Line of Life on the right hand was abruptly broken. I made a rapid calculation, and came to the conclusion that the Italian Monarch was entering a period of danger. Realising that malignant influences from Saturn were culminating, I solemnly warned the King to exercise the utmost prudence in going about, to abstain as far as practicable from journeys, and in fact to be seen as little as possible. He laughed pleasantly.

" Cheiro, I thank you for your warning. I have known for some time that I am as a man sentenced to death." He shrugged his shoulders and concluded: "The welfare of my country stands first." With a few more words we parted.

Barely three months passed, and I was back again in Paris. Then came the terrible news that Humbert had been assassinated while riding in his carriage—a victim of an anarchist. The newspapers were filled with the account of my prediction. Alas; I sorrowed for the brave Italian Monarch cut off thus, but I saw how truly that broken Line of Life in his hand—taken in conjunction with other marks—had warned of his impending doom.

Another very interesting fact is that, when broken in the left hand but joined up in the right, it tells of escape from dangerous illness and likely death.

Sometimes a double Line of Life will be found, as marked in Fig. 19. This inner line is also called the Line of Mars, and indicates great vitality. It is often found in the hands of men of vast physical robustness, joined to great business capacity; some of the greatest captains of industry in the world will be found to have this double line very clearly marked in their palm.

If this Line of Mars is found passing behind the broken Line of Life, it promises that the life will continue, no matter how serious the illness or accident may be.

When the Line of Mars sends an offshoot through the Line of Life, to the opposite side of the hand, as

Missing Page

Page No. 112

indicates a naturally more delicate constitution, and less force of animal magnetism. This explanation will be understood readily by readers when I recall their attention to the fact that one of the most important blood-vessels going from the body to the hand is called the Great Palmer Arch, which carries the blood up to the hand towards the root of the thumb, and carries the circulation back on the other side of the Arch, almost underneath the Line of Life.

It will, therefore, be seen that people who have a weaker constitution are more likely to have this great Palmer Arch narrower in construction than those who have a robust constitution, and a strong circulation of the blood.

This is the reason why, when the Mount of Venus is large and wide on the hand, it gives rise to the idea that it indicates a more passionate animal nature than when this Mount is thin and narrow.

While mentioning this particular point, I must also call attention to the fact that when the Line of Head is curved downwards, instead of running straight across the palm, it indicates the qualities attributed to the Mount of Venus, i.e., those of the imaginative, romantic nature and shows a greater tendency to fall in love than with people who possess the Line of Head running straight across the hand.

If the Line of Life is seen to rise high on the hand, towards the Mount of Jupiter, the subject has more control over himself, and his life is more governed by the ambitious side of his nature. When, however, the Line of Life rises lower down on the palm, more from the Mount of Mars, it gives less control over the temper. When this sign is noticed, especially in the case of young persons, it will be found that they are more quarrelsome, more disobedient, and have less ambition in connection with their studies.

It will thus be seen that every point of this study bearing on character can be reasoned out from a logical standpoint. This places the study upon a higher foundation than when it is considered purely from the superstitious aspect, with which it has so long been associated.

CHAPTER VIII

DAYS THAT ARE SHORTENED

It is a serious and solemn consideration that many individuals shorten their existence by deliberate acts, by rashness, or by a neglect of obvious warnings.

The precious legacy of Life is not given to be squandered. Like the parable of the talents, our gifts—health, mental attainments and opportunities—are lent us that they may be increased. What spectacle can be more beautiful than old age crowned with success, no matter how humble; what more depressing than the failure, who has been above all a traitor to Self.

My great desire in publishing my books, explaining the meaning of the lines and marks upon the hands, is that people may "Know Themselves." I do solemnly believe that those signs graved in the palm are there to be understood; it is lamentably true that only a tiny section of the community do understand them. But I believe that, by means of a simple and concise explanation of every line and its subsidiary marks, great light can be shed upon the problem that agitates every thinking individual: "What are the forces guiding and influencing my life? Can I evade or change Destiny?"

Palmistry is a science that can be made extremely helpful, or, in the hands of the unscrupulous, it can become a snare. I want to bequeath as a legacy to the public the fruits of my twenty-one years active study of Cheiromancy, enriched as it has been by practical illustrations brought under my notice. I have now given up the public profession of the Art, but I still study the science of Palmistry deeply, believing that it holds the key to many problems of human nature that would otherwise be dark.

I have dealt with two characteristic forms of the Line of Life, and its subsidiary markings. I wish now to pass on to the others, and it should be remembered that it is impossible to over-estimate the importance of this. It not only denotes Length of Days; taken in conjunction with the Line of Health (with which I shall deal later), it tells its story of sickness or freedom from physical suffering; also it speaks of threatening disasters, of mysterious overshadowings when the vital power is threatened. No wonder then that the Line of Life was always treated by the ancients with such respect.

I shall now consider two very characteristic formations of this Line that I constantly met in my consulting-room. I append illustrations of them.

When the Line of Life is linked like a chain, as in Fig. 20, or made up of minute pieces, it is a sure sign of delicacy and ill-health that should be carefully guided against. Here can be seen the value of Palmistry, when it can utter its warning note. The weak of chest, the unstable constitution easily upset by excess or strain, the condition where it is dangerous to draw an overdraft upon the Bank of Health—all this can be seen in this particular Line of Life. I may cite a couple of incidents bearing upon this.

As is very well-known, I had the honour of being

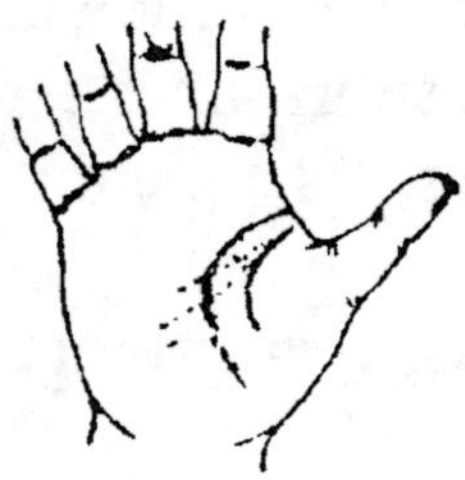

FIG 20.

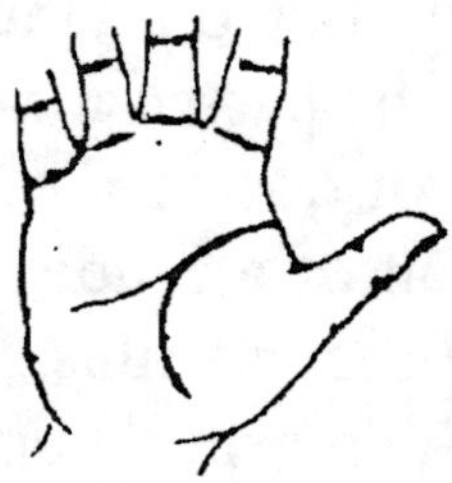

FIG 21.

THE LINE OF LIFE

received by King Edward, when Prince of Wales, and in the library of Marlborough House, he listened with deep attention while I explained to him my system of predicting by numbers.* But before this, I had read his royal hands, under rather disturbing circumstances following a dinner-party given by a distinguished lady, well-known in society. I had no idea who my client was, as he was seated behind a curtain; but I had just mentioned some of the most important dates in his life, when suddenly the curtain fell—and I was face to face with His Royal Highness.

* Publishers' Note: Cheiro's System of Numerology is fully explained in "Cheiro's Book of Numbers."

In his own peculiarly charming way, he begged me not to be discomposed, and we then entered upon a long conversation upon the Line of Life. This was in 1891. He mentioned that he had noticed very particularly that, in the hand of his beloved eldest son, the Duke of Clarence, the Life Line was linked or broken into small fragments. I said that I could not help regarding this as an unfavourable sign. At the time, there was no suspicion that the second heir to the Throne was delicate, but on January 14th, the following year (1892), he passed away after a short illness. In the words of one of the physicians, "he went out like the snuff of a candle."

The second illustration was, if anything, more forcibly imprinted upon my mind.

I was visited in my rooms one day by a rather over-dressed young man, who gave me the impression of being rather "fed up" with life in general. He certainly had brains; that was clearly revealed by his hand; and he had uncommon opportunities vouchsafed by almost unlimited wealth. In fact, rarely have I seen a hand where the indications pointed more to opportunity. Yet the Line of Life on the right hand told me a startling tale.

"From certain indications that I see, I advise you to take the greatest care of your health. Otherwise, I cannot predict for you a long life," I said.

The young man gave a somewhat supercilious smile.

"Don't you worry, Cheiro, I'm as strong as a horse and shall live to be ninety. All our family are long-lived creatures."

I do not know why, but some instinct compelled me to reply with unusual earnestness.

"Be warned by me. Take the most scrupulous care of yourself and avoid excess. If you do, the danger may pass—if not—"

I left the sentence unfinished.

My visitor departed, and it was not long before every newspaper rang with the tale of his mad spending of money, and madder spending of his priceless health. For the young man was Mr. Peter Robinson, who, at the death of his famous father, came into a million pounds and had the immediate handling of it.

As often occurs, he was fastened upon by a swarm of parasites who soon sucked him dry, and during that time, he dissipated at such a pace that at last he was brought down to death's door. Perhaps he thought of my words and made an effort to pull himself together, for I know that, while staying at Maidenhead, at the house found for him by some of the "boys" who were feeding upon his wealth, he did lay off for a time and regained something of his old health. But it was too late; there came a relapse into wild living—and he died "without living out half his days."

I could multiply these examples.

Aubrey Beardsley and Phil May—what two priceless Bohemians these were, who, when they were in the mood, could create artistic gems that still live. I knew them both, and I knew too that both carried the fatal sign in their hands. Phil May, of course, drank so hard that he literally killed himself while still young; Beardsley, after the success of the "Yellow Book" was assured, soon lay in a consumptive's grave.

Sometimes many fine lines are seen, passing from the Line of Life, or from the Line of Mars, towards the opposite base of the palm. Again and again I have proved this to indicate ill-health, brought about by a craving for excitement or intemperance.

In Fig. 21 will be seen another formation of this Line, that is also most significant.

The Line of Life and the Line of Head are seen, as it were, *clinging together* half-way down the palm. This is the sign of a highly-nervous over-sensitive person. With a thin or weak-looking Line of Life, such a person is likely to worry himself into bad health. They are also over-timid, over-cautious, and have little courage in facing the realities of life.

When, on the contrary, the Line of Life and that of Head are only slightly connected, the person will be both sensitive and cautious, but not unduly so.

I recollect on one occasion that there came to my consulting-room a rather timid gentleman, whose "face was indeed sickled o'er with the pale cast of care." He told me that he had inherited from his father a very extensive manufacturing business that demanded a great deal of intricate management. He had been brought up to the business in earlier days, and had mastered the rudiments of it; then he had left it and travelled the world over, giving rein to his artistic nature. Now his father was dead, and in his will he had desired that his son should be given the first option of carrying on the business; if not, it was to be turned into a limited company.

"What would you advise me to do, Cheiro?" he asked.

I noted his characteristic Line of Life, and how easily worry would sap his constitution.

"If you can arrange satisfactory terms, I should advise you to have nothing to do with the business. You are unfitted, and I think that the resulting worry would have a very ill effect upon your health."

He agreed, thanked me warmly, and went away.

But a few days later, I received a letter, in which he wrote that he had had a chat with his solicitor; that the man of Law had expressed the opinion that Palmistry was "all humbug"; in short that he had decided to go against my advice. A postcript in his letter struck my attention:

"I am doing what I am advised is best, yet I have my doubts."

Over twelve months ran their course, when one day I received a letter asking if, "in kindness," I would visit a man whose "days were numbered." It was a request I could not refuse. I drove to an address in Knightsbridge, and in a handsome bedroom I found, propped up by pillows, the gentleman who had visited me.

"Cheiro," he said feebly, and I did not need to be told that the end was quite near, "it is good of you to come, although something told me you would. I disregarded your advice, and I must pay the price. The worry of the business was too much for me; I hung on as long as I could, until a breakdown came. So the sign in the hand was right after all."

Three days later he was dead.

I mention these cases just to show that, too often rashness or obstinacy may bring about disaster that could be avoided with care and proper attention to warnings.

When the Line of Life has the appearance of lying closely into the ball of the thumb, sometimes called the Mount of Venus, thus making this part of the palm look narrow, the physical or vital forces are never robust. Such persons have little or no passion in their love affairs, and, if married, are generally sterile and seldom have children.

The contrary is the case when the Line of Life sweeps out into the palm and makes the ball of the thumb large and prominent.

When the Line of Life has a line ascending from it to the base of the first finger, it is a sign of an ambitious life. Such a person will dictate dan lay down the law, but it is an excellent mark to possess, providing the Line of Head is straight and well marked. Where a woman shows this characteristic, coupled with a *poor* Line of Head, woe to her husband; for she is certain to be a tartar and a law-giver, in the sinister sense that she will be a nagger, and a constant source of trouble to him by her overbearing ways.

I was once much amused by a big and imposing looking man who consulted me in New York, on the eve of his marriage. I judged him to be a weak man, despite his overbearing manners, and I thought he was likely to be rather a blusterer in his own house, provided his wife was a meek creature. He insisted that I should also see his wife to be, and I did so. She was a frail-looking wisp of a creature, and, as the saying is, looked as though she couldn't say boo to a goose. But when I saw her Life Line, I was almost startled. It indicated the iron will—She Who Must Be Obeyed.

I left New York, travelled the country, and was again back in the Capital City. One day the husband, for he was now a married man of some months standing, waited upon me. I saw at once that his crest was strangely lowered.

"Cheiro, I recollect that you warned me as well as you could that I was deficient in will power. You were right. But little did I think that my pride was to be humiliated by a woman, and a little creature at that!"

"You find your wife the Law-Giver?" I ventured.

He groaned.

"Law-Giver! Why, Cheiro, she absolutely rules me. I am not allowed to do anything in my own house. I am a mere worm—and the worst of it is that the neighbours know how matters stand, and I am the laughing-stock of my town."

What could I say. The bride's Line of Life told no lies.

CHAPTER IX

SIGNS THAT ARE SIGNIFICANT

"*The weakling cries: 'O Unkind Fate*
That dashes all my plans to naught.'
The strong will not on Fortune wait;
Thus Self is by Experience taught."

CHEIRO.

IT is a great error to suppose that the Line of Life can be judged solely by itself, or even by its length and depth. It must be studied in conjunction with other signs, and in its relation to the whole hand. It is necessary to examine what I call the subsidiary marks and appearances that accompany it.

I have always looked upon the Line of Life as one of the most highly significant—indeed, the Key Line of the whole hand. But it must be judged with great caution, as an ill-advised reading may cause a great deal of unnecessary suffering.

This was brought home to me, on one occasion, when a lady came to me in great distress. She was obsessed with the idea that she was going to die when she was thirty years of age, and as she was verging upon that age, this "sentence of death" was weighing with terrific force upon her. I asked the reason for the persistent fear that her days were numbered.

"Well, Cheerio," she said, "a short time ago I visited a palmist in a seaside resort, and the woman said emphatically that my Life Line indicated death at thirty."

"I am sorry to hear that," I replied, "but it was, perhaps, a rash verdict."

The shadows seemed to lift from the face of the poor soul as I uttered these words.

"Let me know the worst. I have heard so much of you from various friends, that I feel as if I had perfect faith in your judgment."

I examined her hand. Yes, it was true, that *apparently* her Life Line was broken abruptly at what might reasonably be supposed to be the thirtieth year of her life. But, examining more closely, and taking into consideration other signs that I shall explain in due course, I said emphatically:

"You have before you a long, and, I believe, a happy life."

She clasped her hands with an expression of utter relief.

"Then you think my fears are baseless?"

It was then I told her, as simply as I could, that it appeared to me that danger threatened when she approached her thirtieth year, and that while I did not believe it to be physical, it was certainly some accident that would threaten life.

"You will have a narrow escape," I said, and I added as an afterthought: "Beware of taking a train journey on any Saturday as you enter your birthday month, especially as it is now your thirtieth year."

She thanked me, signed her name in my autograph book, and went her way.

Her case had certainly passed from my mind, when, over a year later, she again entered my consulting-room. But whereas before she had worn the shadow of sorrow, now she seemed to radiate a happiness that I must confess impressed me.

"Cheiro," she said, as she took my hand, "how wonderful you are! The fatal time has passed—and, as you see, I am very much alive. I feel like a person who has been delivered from sentence of death."

Then, sitting down, she told me a curious and interesting story.

"A few days before my thirtieth birthday," she said, "I received a telegram, asking me to go to my mother who was in Glasgow. I knew she had been ailing, and was distressed with the thought that she might be worse. I determined to go at once and wired that I was coming. When I got to Euston, I was on the point of taking my ticket, when suddenly I recollected that it was a Saturday. Almost at the same moment a voice seemed to sound in my ears—*your* voice, Cheiro!—warning me, almost entreating me, not to make the journey.

"But I thought of my mother, and how stupid people would think me if I stayed away because of a 'voice.' I have always found it hard to bear ridicule, so I pressed forward again to the ticket-window. But now, in a most extraordinary fashion, something seemed to bar me from the window. I wanted to go, but something held me back. Cheiro, it seemed to me that you were there, invisible, preventing me from rushing upon my Fate. I did not go. I wired to my mother that I could not come, and a message came back to say that she was better. But that train was wrecked in a disastrous accident, and many people were killed and maimed. Nearly all of them were in the front of the train—it has always been my habit to travel in that part of the train."

I pass by this story without comment, except to emphasise how a real knowledge of the many lines of the hands, and the subsidiary marks, enables one to advise against malignant influences that threaten. *Lines may appear, diminish, or fade*—a fact that must always be borne in mind when reading the hand. The duty of the true student of the Occult, therefore, is to warn the subject of approaching danger by pointing out evil tendencies or threatening aspects that might lead to disaster. No single evil mark should be accepted as decisive. If the evil is important, almost every chief line will show its effect, and both hands must be consulted before the decision is accepted as final.

A line on one hand may show the *tendency*; when, however, the sign is repeated by other lines, the danger is then a *certainty*.

One of the most important questions ever asked in my consulting-room was:

"Cheiro, can people avert or avoid danger or disaster predicted in the hand?"

My answer always was:

"Yes, most decidedly I believe that they can; but I say just as decidedly that they rarely do so."

I have known hundreds of cases, in my own experience, where people were given accurate warnings which they did not realise until too late. "Too late!" Is there any more dreary phrase heard in the annals of human life.

The most remarkable case of this I can recall was that of a woman whose name I cannot disclose, but I may record that she was extremely well known in London society. She consulted me, and from certain signs in the Line of Life, and other indications, I warned her of an accident caused by animals which would happen at the very point of age she had then reached. She looked incredulous, and then, after considering my words, promised that she would use the utmost caution. As she left me, I again emphasised this need for caution, for her case made a very particular impression upon my mind.

A week later it was a dark, foggy night. She ordered out her magnificent pair of bay horses.

But again she was warned—this time through her husband, who begged her not to go out, as the horses were restive and the night so bad. She laughed, and insisted that the high-mettled animals should be brought round.

One more warning came.

Her coachman was taken seriously ill, and a substitute had to be found. Even this did not deter her, and she started out through the murky night. The coachman could have gone four different ways to reach his destination—by a strange chance, he took the most unlikely and drove through Bond Street. The coachman lost control of the horses, they dashed madly on to the sidewalk, and smashed the carriage against a lamp-post. By an amazing coincidence, the injured lady was carried into my hall. She lingered a short time, and then died.

The above is only one example of many that could be cited, to show that we should ever go by warnings, no matter in what way they may be given.

Sometimes a hand discloses the Lines of Heart, Head, and Life all joined together. It is invariably a sign of some great catastrophic end to a career that might have been promising if there had been more self-control.

I recollect once, while in Paris, that a strikingly handsome man entered my consulting-room and announced himself as a grandee of Spain. He said that he had heard I had predicted for some very high personages, and wished me to examine his hands. I did so with interest, for he was obviously a man of breeding and great charm.

If ever a man was dowered by the gods with great gifts, it was this man. An artist to his finger tips; musical; a real lover of Nature—to the gifts of his mind, he had added the polish of education and travel. Yet, like the young man in the Scriptures, there was "one thing lacking."

I saw not only an utter lack of self-control in love, indicating a tempestuous love affair of no ordinary character, but there was plainly indicated a denouement of a terrific character, that would lead to the death of one, if not two people.

As guardedly as I could, I warned him of his fatal lack of self-control, and that, unless checked, its results must be deplorable. He listened thoughtfully, stroking his small black moustache.

"Monsieur Cheiro, it is true as you say that I am liable to fits of passion, and have been from my boyhood. But now I am in love—ah, how much! with a ravishing angel, and for her sake I shall control myself. Yes, Monsieur, for the sake of my Juliette, I shall root out this detestable vice."

He left, and in the round of my exacting profession he had passed from my mind, until, one evening, while dining in one of Paris's most exclusive and *chic* restaurants, I was told by a friend that the sensation of the evening was to be the appearance of Juliette, the Flame Dancer, who was to grace the after-dinner cabaret performance. While

I was digesting this information, I noticed, sitting at another table, the Spanish grandee of whom I have written.

He was alone, brooding, and seemingly ill at ease. But when Juliette, a gorgeous young Spanish woman, clad in a daring costume, appeared at the far end of the restaurant and blew kisses to the company, the young Spaniard was as a man transformed. His whole soul seemed to glow in his eyes, and when Juliette danced between the long array of tables, I noticed that she bestowed her most ardent glances upon the watchful Spaniard.

" A case of a love attachment," I observed to my friend. An old hand at Parisian night life, knowing every one there was to know, he did not answer for a moment or two. Then he said slowly:

" Um, yes, I suppose so. But Juliette has broken so many hearts that I am wondering what will happen, when Prince——"—mentioning the name of my visitor—" discovers that he is not the only pebble on the Parisian beach."

" Then Juliette is a flirt?" I inquired.

" Hardly! Say rather a destroyer of men. Her character is pretty well known to everyone—except to the infatuated Prince. But in his case, of course, love is blind. In Madrid, a man blew out his brains for her; in Lisbon, a friend poisoned himself rather than face disgrace, for he had stolen Government funds in order to provide her with costly gifts. However, the Prince may get over his infatuation."

About a month later, Paris seethed with gossip concerning a carefully hushed up affair that had occurred in this very restaurant. It was said that a Spanish Prince had entered the cabaret and had shot at Juliette, slightly wounding her. He had been arrested, but upon representations from a high quarter, he had been released and hurried over the Spanish frontier. Then had come the startling sequel.

On arriving at his ancestral home, some distance from Madrid, he had retired to his rooms. Ordering the blinds to be drawn, he had surrounded his bed with tall wax tapers. These were lighted by the trembling servants, who were commanded, on pain of his heavy displeasure, to withdraw. Presently the watchers heard the strains of soul-melting music—the heart-vibrating music of Schubert, himself the despairing lover—floating through the corridors.

The Prince had an organ in his room, and was passionately fond of playing. But as the liquid sounds stole through the air, the head butler—a time worn servant of the family, guessed its meaning. The music had ceased long before the heavy door could be battered down; but, on entering, they found the Prince stretched upon the bed, poisoned by his own hand, with Juliette's portrait upon his heart.

When there is a double Line of Life, it denotes excess of vitality. This formation is also called the Line of Mars with which I deal elsewhre.

All tiny lines that rise from the Line of Life are marks of increased gains and successes. They may be called the milestones of the triumphant life.

If such lines ascend towards, or run into the Mount of Jupiter, beneath the base of the first finger, it will denote a rise in position, or a step higher at the date it leaves the Line of Life.

I have examined the hands of scores of men who have made conspicuous success in business and other spheres—men such as Mr. Gordon Selfridge and Sir Edward Marshall-Hall, K.C.—and have pointed out to them this characteristic indication. I have noted, too, this mark as being conspicuous on the hands of great statesmen, such as Mr. Gladstone, "Joe" Chamberlain, Sir Austen Chamberlain, all of whose hands I have had the honour of examining.

But if the lines, on the contrary, rise to Saturn—that is, beneath the second finger—and follow by the side of the Line of Fate, it denotes the increase of wealth and worldly things, but resulting from the subject's own energy and determination.

If such a line leaves the Line of Life, and ascends to the Mount of the Sun—that is, beneath the third finger—it denotes distinction according to the class of the hand. Thus, in the hand of Lord Russell of Killowen, who became Lord Chief

Justice of England, I found this significant sign, and I told him, long before the greatest forensic honour came to him, that he would one day rise to the topmost height in his particular profession. He noted down carefully what I told him, and on the day that he was first robed as Lord Chief Justice, he sent for me to come to his rooms at the Law Courts, that he might congratulate me.

If it leaves the Line of Life and crosses to Mercury, it promises great success in business or science—again in accordance with the class of hand, whether square, spatulate or conic. This is quite easy to understand if a little reflection is given to the subject. For instance, such a line on the square hand would indicate success in business or science; on the spatulate hand, in invention or discovery; and on the round or conic, it would foretell success in money matters, reached by the impulsive action of such a nature, as in sudden speculation or enterprise.

I have found that when the Line of Life divides towards the end, and a wide space is left between the lines, it is an indication that the subject will most probably end his life in a country different from that of his birth—or at least there will be some great change from the place of birth to the place of death.

An island on the Line of Life means an illness or loss of health, while the island lasts. On the other hand, a clearly-formed island at the commencement of the Line of Life denotes some mystery connected with the person's birth.

What subject can be more fascinating than disputed paternity, especially when it involves a change in the Peerage, or some story of a "changeling child." In the consulting-room of the professor of the Occult some odd cases occur—perhaps I should say that the fringe of a mystery is lifted, but discretion forbids it being raised altogether.

I remember a society lady bringing her charming daughter to see me on one occasion. I noticed that the girl's hand bore this significant sign, but I made no remark upon it. A few days later, the mother came to see me alone, and adopted a rather haughty and sneering tone, as if to suggest that I was merely an impostor.

"Really, Cheiro, I fear you have been much over-rated. Nothing that you have told me seems out of the ordinary."

I must own that the words stung me, and I threw discretion to the winds.

"Madam," I retorted, "if you desire absolute candour, I can let you have it, although for your own peace of mind I have kept silent. Is there not a vital secret in your life?"

As I said these words, she grew pale, and I felt her hands flutter nervously.

"What do you mean?" she demanded, with an attempt to speak haughtily.

"This," I said simply. "There is a mystery concerning your daughter's birth."

I said no more, for, with a faint shriek, she rose and cried in a shattered tone:

"Cheiro, you are more than human. How do you know these secrets that I thought were buried in the grave, and in my own breast?"

I told her that my art revealed them, that they were safe with me, and that she need have no fear. From that day, the matter has remained buried by discretion, but I have learned that these significant lines cannot err.

CHAPTER X

THE LINE OF MARS

> *"Some flowers are bruised, that they may be more*
> *sweet,*
> *While some lie broken 'neath the rush of feet.*
> *And some are worn awhile, then tossed aside;*
> *Some grace the dead, while others deck the bride.*
> *And so in Life I've seen the saddest face,*
> *The broken flower, give forth the sweetest grace."*
>
> CHEIRO.

THE Line of Mars is sometimes known as the Inner Vital, or Inner Life Line, and it will be seen in the plate marked as the Double Line of Life. It must not be confounded with an attendant line, which springs off or out of the Line of Life itself.

Mars, of course, was the god of war in mythology, therefore this line indicates everything relating to vitality, or the fighting and striving instinct of the subject. Men who have been great strivers, who will fight to the last ditch as it is said, will almost always be found to have this sign upon their hand. Napoleon was keenly interested in the Occult, and discussed palmistry many times with the Abbe Fornqonville, who accompanied him on his victorious campaign in Italy and also to Egypt. The

Abbe relates in his "Memoirs" that he had the honour of examining the hands of the Little Corporal. He thus describes them:

"They were broad and square, the most capable hands I ever saw, the hands of the practical man, who was also a born fighter. I particularly noticed the Inner Line of Life, and pointed out to Napoleon the significance of this. I also discreetly mentioned that there was indicated not only a world-conquest by this son of Mars, but also a great robustness and vitality. He seemed pleased, and asked if Venus was well represented. I thought it wise to be discreet and replied, 'Yes.' He laughed."

As showing how ancient is this often-derided science of Palmistry, it may be mentioned that Aristotle was familiar with it, and frequently referred to it. The Inner Line of Life he characterised as "significant of abounding vitality," and applied it to several of the great generals of his age.

If this line runs very close to the Life Line, it denotes that the individual will be engaged in many disputes and quarrels, and will have a love of litigation. I have had many striking proofs of the truth of this.

On one occasion, a small, sharp-looking man called upon me, and said that he desired my opinion on his hands. I saw that this characteristic was very strongly marked—more so, I think, than I have ever noticed before. I told him some general things concerning himself, and he acknowledged them to be right. I then went on :

" You are extremely apt to get into litigation, and although you know nothing professionally of the Law, you are always being mixed up with solicitors."

He acknowledged this to be right, and inquired if there was anything else of this nature I could tell him. I made another examination, and said :

" Yes, you will engage in a long and heart-breaking litigation with a person very near to you—I believe it is your wife ; you will have frequent opportunities and warnings to drop it. But your impetuous fighting character will carry you on, and ultimately it will be your ruin."

He laughed loudly.

" Well, Cheiro," he said boastingly, " I do not think much of your predictive powers. No one will ever beat me !" He tapped his chest arrogantly. Then he told me that he was embarking upon litigation with his wife's brother, concerning some property he alleged was due to her.

" Does your wife approve of this action at law ?" I inquired.

" No," he said quickly. " She has no head for business, and is altogether too soft and tender to fight for anything. But I do not trouble about that. What is hers is mine, and I intend to fight for it."

It was as I had surmised. The husband was a blustering fighter, caring not whether he rode rough shod over everybody else so long as he attained the end. The wife was a meek little creature, with no will of her own, or what will she had was submerged in that of her "lord and master."

I could not help saying:

"I suppose your wife yields to you submissively in all these matters?"

"Oh, yes," he said carelessly, "she's what they call a model wife. I've made her one."

The words I have placed at the head of this chapter represent my feelings concerning these "flowers" of life, that are indeed bruised and broken beneath the feet of hardier natures. Though crushed, they give forth the sweet perfume of a gracious character. I pass on to the sequel.

It must have been about two years later that this gentleman called upon me again. But what a change there was in his outward appearance! I could not help noticing that his old confident demeanour had given place to a far more subdued air. Without any preliminaries, he said:

"Cheiro, I come to you a broken but a wiser man."

"You have had trouble?" I said gently.

"I am a ruined man," was the response, and then, with a slight flash of the old fire and accompanied by a wry smile, he added: "and through my own pig-headedness. Yes, Cheiro, if I had but taken your advice"—for I had warned him that disaster was marked upon his hand as the result of litigation—"I should be a rich and happy man to-day."

Encouraged by a few words of sympathy, he went on:

"I was advised by my solicitor that my case against my wife's brother was ill-founded and could not succeed. In a passion, I threw him up and sought out a fresh lawyer. He commenced a fresh action, although my wife begged me not to persevere with it, as it was estranging her from all her relatives. I told her to mind her own business which was my business. Well, I lost the action, after a frightful bill of costs, and decided to appeal.

"My solicitor told me frankly that he thought I had not the ghost of a chance. What madness, or amazing perversity possessed me, I cannot say —except that it must be explained by the lines you pointed out on my hand. I jeopardised my business to raise fresh funds, and launched an appeal. It failed! Then came my crowning stroke of folly.

"I told my lawyer that I should appeal to the House of Lords. He threw up his hands in dismay at my foolishness, but I was adamant and he then said that he could not, for the sake of his professional reputation, continue to act for me. I told him with a curse to return the papers.

"I then found another lawyer—a shady attorney who was simply out to fleece me. He piled up an enormous bill of costs, and eventually the case was heard before the supreme tribunal. It failed, and I was buried beneath an avalanche of expenses, devised most cunningly by my legal 'adviser.' On the day that I had to file my petition in bankruptcy, my wife died. Strange, but until then I had not realised her value or her sweet nature."

My client buried his face in his hands.

These are some of the poignant dramas of human life that have passed before my notice. A striving nature is good in its place, when accompanied by clear judgment and prudence. But without these qualities, it is a snare that leads to disaster. I am happy to record that my client pulled himself together after his troubles, and built up a fresh and prosperous business.

This particular line, duplicating the Line of Life, is often found with striking clearness on the hands of men who have risen to very commanding positions, but who have been exposed to great forces of opposition against which they have prevailed.

In other works I have dealt with my momentous interview with the great Lord Kitchener, when, in 1890, I predicted that he would meet his end by drowning. When I examined his hands, I could not help being struck with the fact that they were not only the hands of a fighter—broad and powerful—but that Mars was fully developed, indicating the strong man who would fight as a professional soldier and fight also because he was by nature a "bull-dog." Everybody knows that, again and again, through his career, Lord Kitchener was opposed by politicians, statesmen, and those who disagreed with his policy and methods. But he went steadily on his way, crushing down opposition like the car of Juggernaut—masterful, overbearing perhaps, but a true son of Mars. In his case, joined to this power, was a steady judgment that prevented any ill-advised plunging into schemes that were bound to lead to disaster.

On a thin, narrow hand, I do not regard a secondary Line of Life so good a sign as on the broad and powerful hand. True it supports even the most delicate-looking Life Line, helping the subject by its excess of vitality over breaks, islands, or all marks of ill-health. There is, however, almost always an accompanying irritability of temperament, that involves such a person in constant quarrels with friends and neighbours. Such people rarely make happy husbands or wives; they are inclined to be naggy, and grow sour as age advances.

When a heavy branch shoots out from this Line of Mars to the base of Luna, it is also the sign of a disposition to intemperance and a craving for drugs. Strange, and indeed wonderful, that the hand can thus bear its eloquent warnings; how valuable this knowledge is, when properly used, is well illustrated by the following case that I have drawn from my personal experience.

One afternoon, I was waited upon by a charming

lady, who told me that she had been recommended to me by a dear friend, Lady Paget. My caller had a remarkably clever hand, and I judged her to be a lady of a sympathetic and ardent nature. There was every indication that her life would be happy and prosperous, except for one menacing sign, that I could not pass over after I had finished my examination.

"You have," I said, "a hand that is full of promise. Indeed, I have rarely seen a hand that made so favourable an impression upon my mind. But I must warn you that you have a predisposition, arising out of a fearless nature, to sample every sensation in life. Beware lest this love of adventure should lead you into a habit that may be difficult to break. For if it once grips you, there is every indication that your nature will prove a fruitful soil."

She wrinkled her brow.

"Cheiro," she said at length, "I really do not quite understand you. What precisely is this against which you are warning me?"

I pointed out to her, and explained the meaning of the heavy branch line that shot out in the manner I have indicated.

"That," I said, "is a warning that there may be a hidden weakness in your nature. It should make you doubly careful!"

I felt that she was convinced and the matter dropped. After I had predicted her marriage within a year, she took her leave.

On my return from my successful New York and American visit, I was informed that a Mrs. C. wished to see me very urgently. Her address was given at a high-class nursing home. I was thoroughly perplexed; I knew no Mrs. C., and could not imagine why she wanted to see me. But in the course of my professional career, I have had many inexplicable messages, and have seldom disregarded them. In due course I presented myself at the nursing home and asked to see Mrs. C.

It was my former client, who told me that she married as I had predicted that she would. Her presence in the nursing home was fully explained by the story she told me.

She said her marriage had proved a happy one, but unfortunately her husband, a young diplomat, had to be away a great deal. Left to her own devices, she got in with a very fast set of modern girls, and the whirl of life brought her into some strange places.

"One night, Cheiro, I accompanied two young girls—neither were twenty years of age—to the luxurious studio of a wealthy Bohemian, who posed as a patron and lover of the Arts. After supper, the party degenerated into a wild 'rag.' After we had quieted down a bit, cocaine was handed round in a silver shell. To my amazement, I saw the two young girls take a pinch of the 'snow,' and snuff it up with the greatest zest. I demurred, and my refusal was received with shouts of derision

I was told that everybody took it, and that its effects were perfectly marvellous. Indeed, when I looked at the two young girls, it was really astonishing to see the effect the 'snow' had had upon them. Their pinched and jaded looks had given place to sparkling eyes and rosy cheeks; they corruscated with a new brilliance. My curiosity was piqued.

"Curiosity! Yes, it was true, as you said of me, Cheiro, that the love of adventure was in my blood. I decided that I would sample this new society sin, and I did so. I was astounded at the rush of energy and happiness that followed the first sniff. I will not weary you with details, but in a few months I was a dope fiend, and had passed through all the stages common to this soul and body destroying habit. There came a time when I left home, and buried myself in obscure lodgings in South London, so that I might indulge the craving. For days I would lie in bed unwashed and neglected, lost to all sense of decency, too enervated to care. There came a day when I was discovered by a friend of my family—a man who was always a clever doctor. He rescued me from the frowsy lodgings, tended me, and brought me into this nursing home. After a hard struggle, I have won through, and am my normal self again."

I was much touched by this story. My former client was thin and wasted; it was sad to see how she had altered. I began to express my gladness that she had been able to stem her inclinations in time, but she interrupted me.

"Cheiro," she said, "there was a moment when I felt that I must give up. It was after I was brought here. Everything seemed so hopeless. I felt that I should never have the strength to fight the accursed vice that was destroying me. But suddenly the words you had spoken came into my mind, and seemed to acquire fresh significance. I determined that I would not be beaten, and from that hour strength seemed to be given me to fight the good fight."

CHAPTER XI

THE LINE OF HEALTH

THE Line of Health, known to the ancients as the Hepatica, is one that may well be considered in connection with the Line of Life. It is a line of great interest and importance—and when examining a hand, it is one fraught with the greatest significance. I am well aware that Palmistry is not taken seriously by many members of the medical profession—though a notable exception to this is America, where many doctors and medical students attended my lectures, and acknowledged that they obtained great advantage from them.

Now it is said that to be forewarned is to be forearmed. In ordinary affairs of life, as a matter of common precaution, we protect ourselves against threatened dangers. How much more necessary it should be to guard against dangers that may sever the very thread of life itself. For I can prove conclusively that many fatal illnesses have been writ upon the palm; through the years, disease has slowly but insidiously gained strength, until the ominous words "too late!" are uttered by the physician. Health is indeed the first wealth, and should be guarded by every possible care. That is why I regard a study of the Hepatica or Health Line as being of such supreme importance.

First as to the position of this line.

The Line of Health begins under the little finger and goes down the palm towards the Line of Life. This is clearly illustrated in Fig. 22. (Page 153.)

There has been very considerable discussion among students of this subject as to the part of the hand on which the Line of Health commences.

My own theory, one that I have proved by over twenty-five years' experience, and also watching its growth on the hands of children, is that it rises at the base of or on the face of the Mount of Mercury—and as it grows across the hand and attacks the Line of Life, it foreshadows the development of illness or germ of disease, which, at the date of its coming in contact with the Line of Life, will reach the climax of its attack.

The Line of Life, it must be remembered, merely relates to the promised length of life from heredity and natural causes, but the Line of Health denotes the effect of the class of life the subject has led. The conjunction of these two lines, if one is of equal strength to the other, indicates the date of death.

The Line of Mercury, or of Health, relating as it does to the nervous system, and also to the mind (Mercury), lends itself to the supposition that the all-knowing subconscious brain is cognisant, even at an early age, of the force of resistance in the nervous system. It may know how long this force will last, when it will be exhausted, and consequently may mark the hand long years in advance.

The Line of Health is one of the lines of the hand most subject to changes. It is the thermometer of the life, showing its "rise and fall," as the case may be. I have seen this mysterious line look deep and threatening during the early years of a life, yet completely fade away as greater health and strength took possession of the body.

Again, I have often seen it look deeper and more ominous as the wear and tear, especially of the nervous system, began to make itself manifest, or when the subject over-taxed his mental strength.

Further, it is an excellent sign should this line be absent. Its absence denotes an extremely robust, strong constitution, and a healthy state of the nervous system.

If it rises and seems like a branch from the Heart Line, especially if both these lines are broad in appearance, with the Health Line running across and down the palm, coming in contact with the Line of Life, it is a certain indication of weakness or disease of the heart.

The student should always observe the kind of nails there are on the hand, when thinking out the diseases indicated by the Line of Health.

I shall deal with the nails in the next chapter.

When this Line of Health is very red, in small spots, especially when pressed, rheumatic fever is indicated.

When twisted, irregular, and yellowish in colour the subject will suffer from biliousness and liver complaints.

When found heavily marked, and only joining the Heart and Head Lines together, it foreshadows brain-fever, especially when any islands are marked on the Line of Head.

The Line of Health, running straight down the hand, but not touching the Line of Life, indicates that though the constitution may not be robust, it is wiry, and there is great reserve resistance to disease.

In connection with the examination of the Line of Health, the student must always look for further indications to the rest of the lines of the hand, more especially to the Line of Life and Line of Head. For instance, when the Line of Life looks very chained and weak, the Health Line on a hand will naturally increase the danger of delicate health; when found with a Line of Head full of little islands, or like a chain, such a Health Line clearly foreshadows brain disease, severe headaches, and so on.

By a study of this line the most valuable warnings may be given of approaching ill-health. Whether persons will follow the warnings or not is a question. My experience is that they do not and will not; therefore, whatever is indicated will most probably come to pass.

When the Line of Life round the base of the thumb is made up of little pieces, or linked like a chain, and the Line of Health is thick and heavy, great delicacy and many illnesses may be expected all through life. This is an indication that I have never known to vary. See Fig. 23.

When the Line of Health, or any branch from it, touches the Line of Life, it foretells severe illness and danger of death at the date where the two lines meet. The illustration appended, Fig. 24, illustrates this.

Supposing that the indications are that a severe illness will threaten at forty years of age. Then,

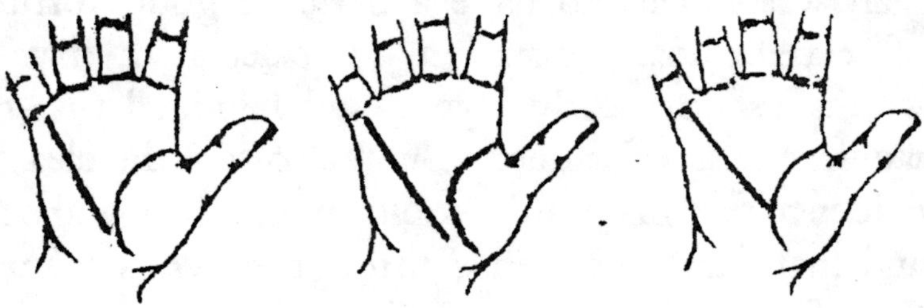

FIG 22. FIG 23. FIG 24.

THE LINE OF HEALTH

warned beforehand, the subject can take all reasonable precautions, especially when it is remembered that a disposition towards various diseases is clearly shown on the human hand. There is the well defined consumptive's hand; the hand exhibiting unmistakeable symptoms of heart weakness for disease; the more sinister signs of brain trouble and weakness, liable to be brought about by overstudy; finally there is the hand shadowing nervous strain, leading under certain conditions to nervous breakdown and neurasthenia, with its many evil complications.

I remember a stout and bustling young man calling upon me one day, and after explaining that he had come for a "lark," he proceeded to display considerable interest in what luck lay before him. He told me that he made a great business of backing horses and playing cards, and I soon gathered that his principal object in visiting me was to see whether a particularly long run of ill luck was likely to be broken.

I found signs that convinced me that this young man was indeed to have a blaze of good fortune of extraordinary duration. I calculated that it would last for nearly a year, and I judged that he would amass a fortune. But I also saw the clearest evidence that his health would suffer a severe shock, and that death threatened through nervous exhaustion, following prolonged dissipation.

"Yes," I said, "your ill-fortune will change with dramatic suddenness. Whatever you touch within the next few months will literally turn to gold. The omens all point to that"—I had ascertained the date of his birth—"for the shadow is rapidly lifting."

He exhibited lively signs of satisfaction at this good news.

"But," I continued, "I must warn you that prosperity often brings its own responsibilities. You must be exceedingly careful how you use your suddenly acquired wealth. Health is like a banking account that may have too many demands made upon it."

He laughed rather scornfully.

"I am as strong as a horse," he said. "I've never had a day's illness in my life, nor felt any ill-effects the morning after the night before. Now that you say I'm to have a lucky period, I'm going to have a real good time."

What use was it to warn headstrong youth. The young man departed, his eyes shining with the expectation of that good time to come. But before he left me, I made one last effort to implant in his mind a sense of caution.

"Yes," I said, "you have indeed a wonderful constitution, but let me remind you of the wise words of the greatest physician of the Georgian Age—Doctor Abernethy: 'Nature never forgets—and never forgives.'"

He looked at me for a few moments and then smiled broadly.

"Good-bye, Cheiro," he said on parting. "If I crack up, I'll send and let you know, so that you may see that your words have come true."

I noted the call down in my book, with a few particulars, and quickly the interview faded from my mind in the press of work. I went to Paris, I had a very successful season there, and once again was in my rooms in Bond Street.

One day I received a telephone call that rather puzzled me.

"Will you go to a nursing home in Bruton Street," said the voice at the other end of the wire.

In reply to my inquiries as to the reason, I could only get the answer that it was " urgent." I decided to go.

When I got to the beautifully-appointed nursing home, I first saw the Matron, who explained that she had telephoned on behalf of a patient who was very ill—in fact, on the verge of insanity.

" You will doubtless have heard of him," she said, " for in almost every newspaper he has been paragraphed as ' The Lucky Plunger '."

Yes, it was true that I had read many flamboyant accounts of this young man's wonderful wins on the turf and at the gaming table, together with his life of extravagance, but I did not connect this with my former caller until I entered the room where he lay in bed. Even then, I recognised with difficulty the emaciated, pallid creature who held out a waxen hand and thanked me for coming.

" Yes, Cheiro," he whispered in a weak voice, " I have kept my word and sent for you, so that you may see that your words have come true. I had my dazzling luck and—I'm going to pay for it. I drew an overdraft on the bank of Health, and the cheques have been referred to drawer—my—self."

I sat down by his bedside and listened while he told me that he " couldn't do wrong " after he had visited me. Horses brought him in thousands, while at Monte Carlo he won day after day. With nearly a hundred thousand pounds in his possession he embarked upon a " glorious time." Women and wine, freak dinners, nights of dissipation, and so forth, had threatened his health with preliminary symptoms that he disregarded. Then there came a sudden collapse. The doctors gravely hinted at general paralysis or insanity.

I am glad to say that, after months of careful nursing, he was pulled out of the Valley of the Shadow of Death. He arose from his sickness a new man—new in body and mind. His fortune was gone, but he set to work with a will and founded a useful business. To-day I have reason to believe that his health is splendid.

How clearly this proves that the hand gave its warning. True, he did not heed it, because he did not understand it. Even when it was pointed out, unbelief prevailed. But by good fortune and good nursing, the danger was averted.

Let me cite a case where the danger was *not* averted.

A lady called upon me on one occasion, and told me that she was going very shortly to the South of France.

"I advise you not to do so," I said.

She looked extremely surprised.

"But surely the South of France in winter is the ideal place for me," she urged. "I cannot stand damp or fog, and the English climate is particularly atrocious just now."

"Will you tell me your exact age?" I countered.

She told me that she was twenty-eight.

Now, I had observed from her Health Line that there was a strong predisposition to sudden attacks of pneumonia or some such complaint, and from a mark on the Life Line, I concluded that my client was entering upon a season when the gravest danger to her health threatened her. Instinctively I guessed that the malignant influences would come upon her while abroad.

"Do not go," I urged. "Stay at home at all costs."

I think my words made an impression upon her, for she said that she would not go. But it is a woman's privilege to change her mind, and later in the afternoon she telephoned that she had mentioned the matter to a friend who had said that it was "all nonsense."

"So, Cheiro, I am going to take the risk," she laughed, and bade me good-bye.

Very shortly she arrived at Nice and plunged into all its gay life. Then one afternoon she decided to have a motor trip up the glorious lower Alps, that form such a lovely background to the Cote D'Azur.

The sun was shining beautifully when she started, but on arriving several thousand feet up, she endeavoured to let down the window of the car in order to get a better view. By a mischance, the glass pane was broken. All the journey home, the piercing wind that blows from these mountains was attacking her. Within a few hours she developed double pneumonia; in four days she was dead.

I did not hear the facts until some months later, when her sister called upon me and mentioned that she had heard of the visit paid to me, and in a letter describing the glorious weather and delights of Nice, my client had written: "I really cannot feel as if I have been condemned to death. Cheiro was wrong."

The Line of Health with a loop or island in it,

FIG 25.

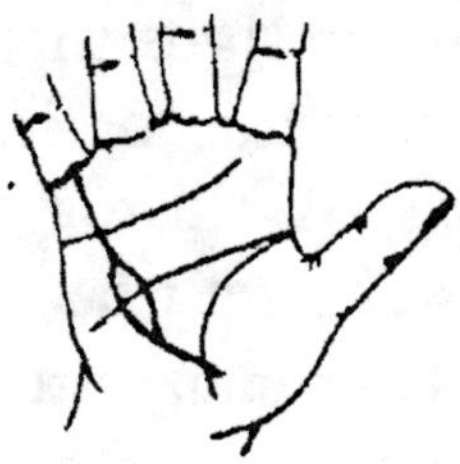

FIG 26.

THE LINE OF HEALTH

near but above the Line of Head, denotes trouble with the nose and throat, and a disposition to catarrh. (See Fig. 25).

The Line of Health forming an island above and below the Line of Head indicates delicacy and danger from the chest and lungs, especially so when the nails are long and almond-shaped. See illustration in Fig. 26.

There may be slight variations of these rules, but in the main they will be found to be sure guides.

As previously mentioned I had the honour of being called to read the hand of King Edward. I noticed how danger threatened from the chest and throat passages of His Majesty; it is, of course, common knowledge that several members of the House of Windsor cannot face the erratic climate of this country in the winter, but must seek warmer climes. I ventured to hint this to the King, and he received it with composure.

"Yes, Cheiro, I am well aware that bronchial catarrh is my enemy and always will be. But you may be sure that I shall fight it to the last."

Reading the signs that I saw on the Royal hand, I felt sure that the conflict at the last would be short and sharp. As history has mournfully recorded, King Edward returned from the Continent practically a dying man, although such was his courage and determination that he endeavoured to make light of it. But the nation was shocked to find, from the grave bulletin issued, that the Peacemaker's days were numbered; he died from heart failure, following bronchial trouble. He had indeed fought to the very last.

Danger of death is clearly indicated when the Line of Life is "broken," and a branch from the Line of Health or the line itself runs into the "break." See Fig. 27.

When the Line of Health appears to turn away from the Line of Life, it denotes complete recovery from whatever illness threatened, and this sign is in itself a promise of a long life. See Fig. 28.

Some people have been much alarmed by being

told by an ignorant student of palmistry that owing to the absence of a Health Line, this is an indication of a short life. On the contrary it denotes an extremely robust, strong constitution, and a healthy state of the nervous system.

If a hand indicates a Line of Health, the best position for it to lie is straight down the hand, not approaching or touching the Line of Life. When found crossing the hand, touching or throwing branches across to the Line of Life, it foretells that

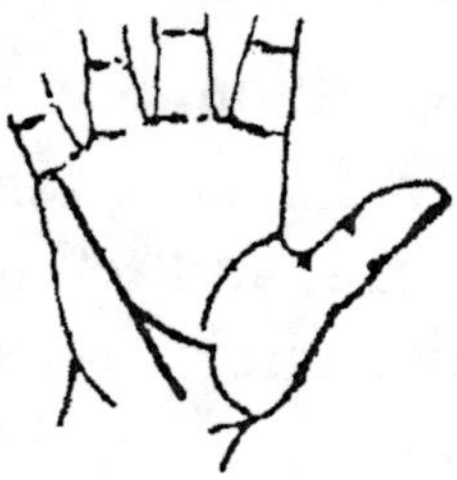

FIG 27.

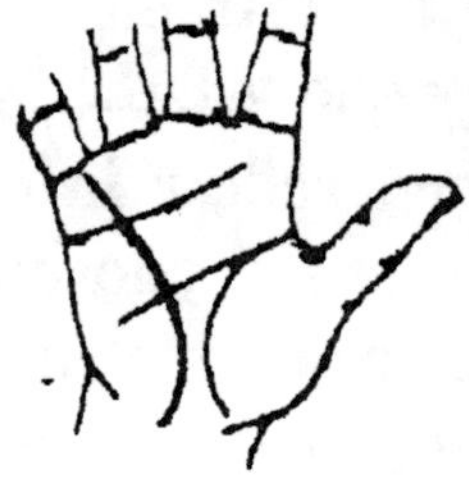

FIG 28.

THE LINE OF HEALTH

there has been some illness at work which is undermining the health.

The late famous theatrical manager, Mr. George Edwardes, visited me on one occasion and I observed these conditions in his hand. He asked me what the length of his days would be, and I replied that, while I saw something that led me to believe that his years were not long, still with care and scrupulous attention to avoid overwork, his days might be lengthened. But his work overwhelmed him, and he died prematurely aged and worn out. Literally, his work had killed him.

Providence has placed warnings and signposts in our hands. Alas, that so often the warning is disregarded!

The lines on the palm should be clearly marked, a good pink or reddish colour, and they should be free from breaks, crosses, holes or irregularities of all kinds.

When very pale in colour, they show lack of force and loss of energy, and often poor health.

When extremely red, they indicate excessive energy and a rather violent disposition.

When yellow in colour, they denote a tendency to biliousness and liver complaints, and tell in consequence of a melancholy morose nature.

Forked lines are generally good, and increase the quality of the special indication. When at the end of the Line of Head, the fork gives more of what is called a dual mentality, and less power of concentration on any one subject. (Special Plate.)

Spots on a line weaken it and arrest its growth.

Tasselled Lines (Special Plate) are not good signs. They weaken any indication the line itself denotes, and at the end of a Life Line, they foreshadow loss of all nervous energy.

Wavy Lines (Special Plate) show uncertainty, lack of decision and want of force.

Broken Lines (Special Plate) destroy the meaning of the line at the particular place where the break appears, but if one line ends above the other, the break is not so bad, and the quality of the line will be continued.

Sister Lines (Special Plate) increase or double the power of any line, and when lying close together at the Line of Head, they give it great power and promise.

Islands (Special Plate) are always evil, and denote

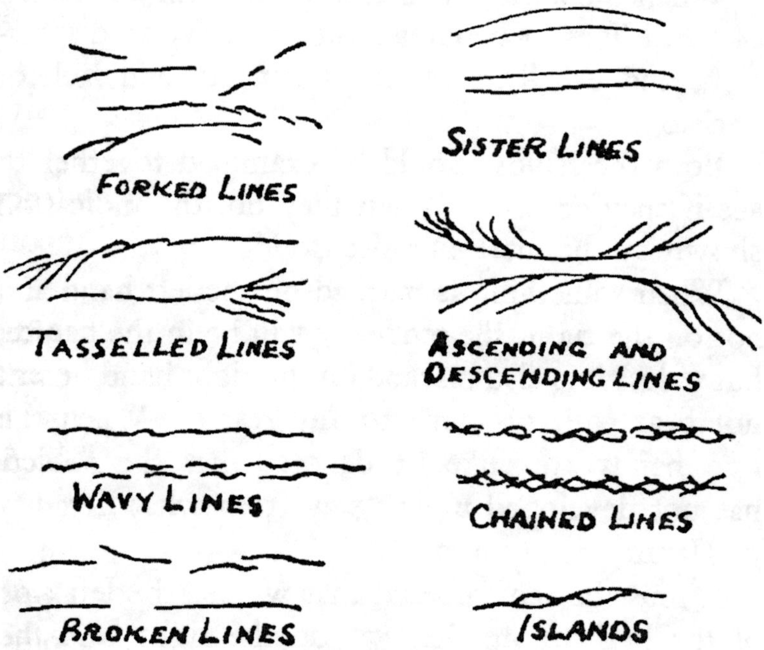

SPECIAL PLATE
MINOR MARKS AND SIGNS

weakness or failure of the Line or Mount on which they may be found.

Ascending Lines (Special Plate) are good from any line from which they spring. From the Line of Life, they denote increased energy wherever they make their appearance. If they run up to any particular Mount or part of the hand, they show that the increased effort or energy will be in that particular direction.

Descending Lines (Special Plate) are the reverse and mean loss of power.

Chained Lines show lack of force or fixity of purpose (Special Plate).

When the entire hand is covered with a network of small lines, it denotes a highly nervous disposition, and usually great mental worry and lack of decision.

Both the hands should be examined together to see if they accord. When they do, the indication shown by the mark is more decided.

When something is marked on the left hand and not on the right, the tendency will be in the nature, but unless it is also marked on the right hand, it will not bear fruit or come to any result. When the two hands are alike, it denotes that the subject has not developed in any way from what heredity or Nature gave to him.

It must be remembered that we use the left side of the brain more than we do the right, and the nerves cross and go to the right hand. Consequently, it is this hand which denotes the developed or active brain, the left only giving the natural tendencies or inclinations.

To be scientific and accurate, the student of this subject must always keep this rule before his mind, and not be led away in his judgment by some " marvellously good line," to which the subject may proudly call his attention in the left hand; such a mark will have no actual result, unless it is also found on the right hand.

History has by now lined up faithfully the follies, the shrewdness and the calculating cleverness in finance and diplomacy, of Leopold the Second, King of the Belgians.

I had the honour of reading his hand, revealing to him his length of years. It was an interesting experience, for Leopold, whom Edward the Seventh dubbed "Spade-beard," was a complex Man as well as a versatile Monarch.

Circling around my memories of Leopold must of necessity come the recollection of two women, with both of whom his name was associated: the Baroness Vaughan, his unrecognised wife, and the sparkling Gaby Delys, with whom Leopold flirted in kingly fashion.

The magnetic personality of this monarch, at the time the most talked of King in Europe, gripped me with intense fascination.

Laeken is a fine-looking palace, originally an old Chateau very much modernised, and surrounded by beautiful woods. I made my way to the main entrance, was stopped by the guard, handed over to an officer, and quickly found that a card given me by the King was an *Open Sesame*. On the stroke of six I was seated in a small room, plainly furnished, and not unlike the sitting-room of an hotel.

Suddenly one of the inner doors opened, and His Majesty appeared; he was dressed very simply in a morning suit, and was smoking his eternal cigar. He bade me come to his study and quickly made me feel quite at home. For some minutes the conversation turned upon the British Royal Family. One remark I can repeat, as it was shrewd: "When King Edward has his 'head' in foreign affairs, he will be a big surprise. He is a born diplomat." He also made some penetrating remarks upon the character of the Duke of York, now King George. I was amazed to see how the Belgian King had studied various Royalties.

"Now, Cheiro," he said, "I want you to examine my hands and tell me what you can. I have heard from several sources of your remarkable skill in predictions of death days, and important dates in life. I want you to tell me of any striking events that you see; anything that portends in the near future."

As he uttered these words, the King's manner became very serious; I felt that he realised that the shadow of "The End" was creeping over his long reign, and that he half dreaded, yet longed, to peer into the "Future all unknown."

With this, he laid his strong masterful hands upon a small cushion, and remained absolutely silent while I made a careful examination of the characteristic lines. Sixty-two years of crowded life seemed indexed on the right palm; while on the left I saw graved the hereditary pointers that told their own tale of the impulses, ups and downs, and the physical weaknesses that are just as visible on the palm of royalty as on any other hand.

As briefly as I was able, I explained that the indications pointed to a strong brain, remarkable lung development, a sound nervous system, while the circulation was above normal. Parenthetically I may state that it is beyond dispute that upon the palm of the hand is graved a chart of health, and later I hope to explain this.

"Quite sound then, Cheiro?" he questioned, fixing his imperious eyes upon my face. I paused, for I saw written there a fatal defect which I realised must soon bring the Royal frame down to the dust of dissolution.

"If there is a weakness," I said diplomatically, "it lies in the digestive system."

"No, no," he countered emphatically. "You are wrong, Cheiro—I can eat anything."

I let it pass and went on to other matters, but when two years later, on the 17th December, death called for the King at his Palace, the official bulletin gave the cause of dissolution as a complete breakdown of the digestive organs and bowel obstruction.

Quite early in my career I read the hand of "Joe" Chamberlain; later Sir Austen, his son, allowed me the same privilege, and I should like to emphasise a remarkable parallel in the lines on the hands of father and son.

One evening I was at the house of Mrs. Walter Palmer, in Mayfair, when she desired that I should read the hands of some of the guests. The first who impulsively offered his palm for inspection was "Joe" Chamberlain. His lines were very decisive, and the Line of Sun or Success was marked, rising boldly and never faltering. But I could not help noticing the ominous sign of the Hepatica or Health Line.

At a position showing danger in the region of the sixty-fifth year, there were clear indications of a sudden collapse from mental overstrain, and I hinted at this as guardedly as possible.

"Joe" brushed this aside impatiently, although of course it is a matter of political history that in the zenith of his Tariff Reform campaign, he was suddenly struck down by paralysis, finally ending his brilliant career after a lingering illness.

"Joe" Chamberlain said to me:

"I am very anxious about the career of my son Austen. If I obtain a print of his hand, will you read it for me?" I agreed.

In due course it arrived, and I saw the father. I explained broadly the indications upon the hand of the son as follows:

"He will fill some of the highest positions in Parliamentary life. It appears to me that the zenith of his career will be in 1925. In that year he will secure a great international triumph; he will one day be a Leader of the House of Commons."

These predictions were written down by "Joe," and I have reason to know that they were found carefully treasured at the time of his death.

Since those words were uttered, Sir Austen Chamberlain has been Postmaster-General, Leader of the House of Commons, Foreign Secretary, and acclaimed as one of the main authors of the Treaty of Locarno.

But it is somewhat ominous to see that, in the hand of Sir Austen, there is the same tendency in the Line of Health as was found upon the Health Line of his father. It most certainly indicates a tendency towards overtaxing the mental and physical strength, with a possibility of collapse. Sir Austen should be extremely careful to avoid overstrain and undue fatigue, or the consequence in his fifty-six to sixtieth years may be dangerous.

CHAPTER XII

HEALTH AND THE HAND

WHILE considering the Line of Health and all that it conveys of the bodily state and the physical characteristics, the nails must not be overlooked. Experience has taught me that the nails of the hand are remarkably indicative, and can illustrate very wonderfully the internal conditions that might even escape the eye of the physician.

This section of Palmistry is now recognised by the majority of medical men, who seldom fail quietly to observe the appearance of the nails on a patient's hand.

They are peculiarly indicative of hereditary diseases, especially lungs, heart, nerves, and spine.

They are divided into four very distinct classes. Long, Short, Broad, and Narrow.

When the nails are found very long, the general constitution never appears to be so strong as when they are medium in size.

Persons with long nails are more liable to all diseases of the Lungs and Chest and still more so when these long Nails are seen ribbed or fluted, with the ribs running upward from the base to the edge of the nail.

The same type of nail, but shorter in appearance, indicates that the delicacy lies higher up towards the throat, and denotes tendencies for laryngitis, inflammation of the throat and all bronchial troubles.

When specially long nails are bluish in colour, they denote a still more delicate constitution, coupled with poor circulation of the blood.

Nails short in appearance denote a tendency towards weak action of the heart, more especially so when the "moons" are very small or barely noticeable. When the nails appear very flat and sunk into the flesh at the base they denote nerve diseases. When they are "ribbed" across the nail from side to side, the danger is still more apparent.

When a deep furrow is found across the nail, it is a sign in any hand that an unusual call has recently been made on the nervous system by illness. If the following rule is studied, the date of this illness or strain can be very clearly indicated.

As it takes about nine months for a nail to grow out from the base to the outer edge, the nail can easily be divided into sections. When the furrow or very deep "rib" is seen close to the edge, the illness took place about nine months ago; when the furrow is seen about the centre, the date was about from four to five months, and when at the base, about one month previously.

White spots on the nails are a sign of general delicacy, and when the nail is seen covered with small white flecks, the whole nervous system is in a low state of health.

Very narrow nails show spinal weakness, and when extremely curved and very thin, they indicate curvature of the spine and great delicacy of the constitution.

When the nails appear very flat and inclined to lift themselves up from the flesh towards their outer edge, the threatened danger is towards paralysis, and still more so when they look like a shell and are pointed towards the base. When these nails are without any signs of moons, whitish or bluish in colour, the disease is in a very advanced stage.

Large " Moons " always denote strong action of the heart and rapid circulation of the blood, but when unusually large, they indicate much pressure on the heart, rapidity in its beat, the valves overstrained and danger of bursting some blood vessel in the heart or in the brain.

Small " Moons " indicate the reverse of this; they always denote poor circulation, weak action of the heart and anæmia of the brain.

When close to death, the " Moons " are the first to take on a bluish look, while later on, the entire nail becomes blue or almost black in colour.

I shall now discuss these points in details, with examples, from my own long personal experience with clients of all classes.

I always remember the gratitude of a mother who brought her daughter, a charming and vivacious girl, to see me. She appeared to be a picture of health, but I discerned this sinister sign of threatening consumption. I did not hesitate to warn the mother, and although at first she was incredulous, as "It was not in the family" and "never had been," she afterwards agreed to guard the girl during the winter.

I lost sight of her for some time, until she called one day and related that the first winter had been spent in Egypt; the second she had neglected to send her child away. A simple cold developed rapidly into alarming symptoms, until a famous physician was called in and advised immediate change in Egypt. This prompt action undoubtedly saved the girl's life, for she became quite well. The physician said afterwards that he was surprised how suddenly the threat of the disease had made itself manifest. If the mother had not had her mind prepared by my warning, she might have neglected too late the change of climate. I could multiply such cases many times over.

The son of a Colonel who was a promising member of the Secret Service, called upon me one day, and I saw at once a strong disposition to this fell disease. I told him so; too bluntly, perhaps, for he appeared offended and muttered that I was not a physician. I would not allow myself to take offence at this, but warned him most earnestly to avoid taking cold; but if he did take a chill, he must use every means to throw it off.

"Cheiro, I have wonderful health. What you are saying is nonsense."

"Then," I could not help saying, "you will rush on to your Fate, and perhaps will remember my warning too late."

Barely a year elapsed before I received a visit from a broken-hearted father. He was bowed with sorrow, and told me that his boy had died of consumption—rapid decline of the most virulent kind. He had scoffed at "coddling," and had always said that his health was perfect. A neglected cold suddenly provoked the advance of one of Nature's most dire diseases.

Many people imagine that long nails indicate great physical strength, and that short ones show the reverse. This is a delusion, as I have many times proved. Very long nailed persons are more liable to suffer from weakness and affections of the chest, together with congestion of the lungs and air passages; if the nails are particularly curved in shape, the trouble is likely to be accentuated.

The fluting or rib-like appearance of the nails also has a close connection with the health of the subject.

Chest sufferers nearly always have fluted nails. It would be very interesting if, in hospitals devoted to particular diseases, an examination could be made of the nails of the sufferers. I am convinced that some extremely interesting and suggestive data could be gathered. Again, I emphasise that to be forewarned is to be forearmed. A tendency, either inherited or developed in early life, to a particular disease can be checked if taken in time.

Long nails, very wide at the top and bluish in appearance, denote bad circulation, proceeding from nervous prostration or heart-weakness. This is very often the case with the hands of women between the ages of fourteen and twenty-one, or forty-two and forty-seven.

Turning to a consideration of short, small nails, it is noticeable that these sometimes run in families, in which there is a tendency towards heart-disease. I had a curious illustration of this brought to my notice while in New York.

One afternoon a gentleman called to see me. He seemed extremely concerned about his length of days, and asked innumerable questions concerning his health, but at the same time emphasised that he was as "strong as a horse." Indeed to outward appearance his frame and well-coloured face seemed impressive; he was insistent that he had never had a doctor in his life.

"Now, Cheiro," he said persuasively, although I caught a wistful undercurrent in his voice, "you are going to tell me that I shall be a centenarian."

I asked his age.

"Fifty-five, and good for another fifty."

But words mean nothing, and too often they mask a latent anxiety. I saw that this gentleman had certain signs in his hand, accentuated by his peculiarly short nails.

"Has any member of your family—your father or mother, for instance—died very suddenly?"

"Why do you ask me?" he asked in a low tone.

"Because I have an impression, nay, I may say a certainty, that sudden deaths have not been unknown in your family," I replied.

He hesitated for a few moments.

"You are right. My father dropped dead from heart failure, although I never knew him to have a day's illness. My paternal grandfather also went off like a snuffed candle."

"So you have been haunted with fears . . " I suggested.

"God knows I have. Yes, Cheiro, I came to you to know whether there was anything in my hand that would lead you to believe that such a tragic ending was in store for me. I am rich, I have built up three successful businesses; I have a good wife and several fine sons. Now I want to retire and enjoy life, but there is this shadow of fear hanging over me. Can you dissipate it?"

I told my client candidly that there was a strong disposition to heart-failure; that the Line of Life showed that a crisis was arriving at no distant hour. I said further: "Take the greatest care to avoid exertion, and particularly excitement. If you do, I see no reason why you should not live to a ripe old age."

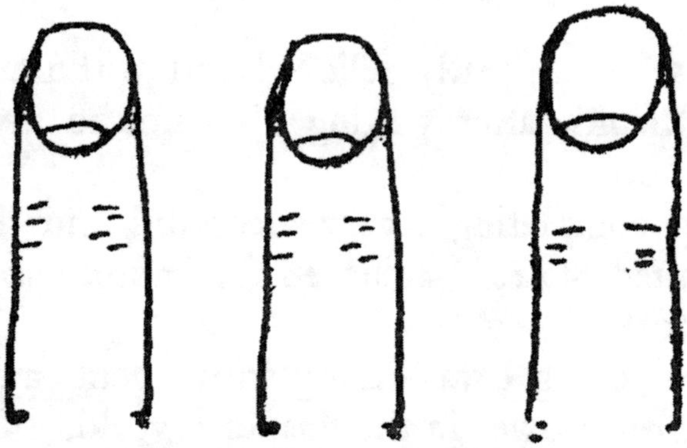

HROAT AFFECTIONS AND BRONCHIAL

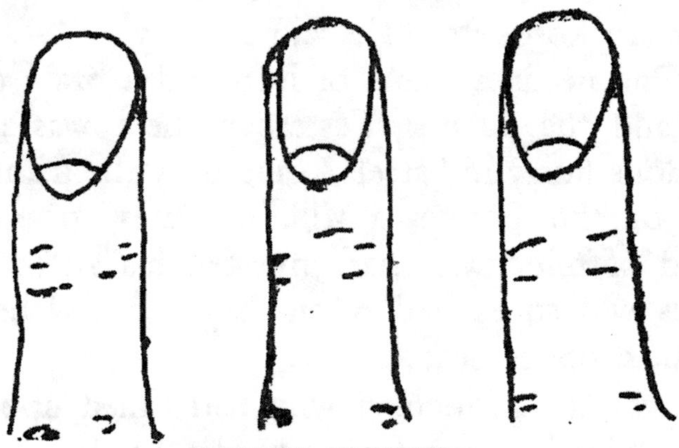

DELICACY OF LUNGS

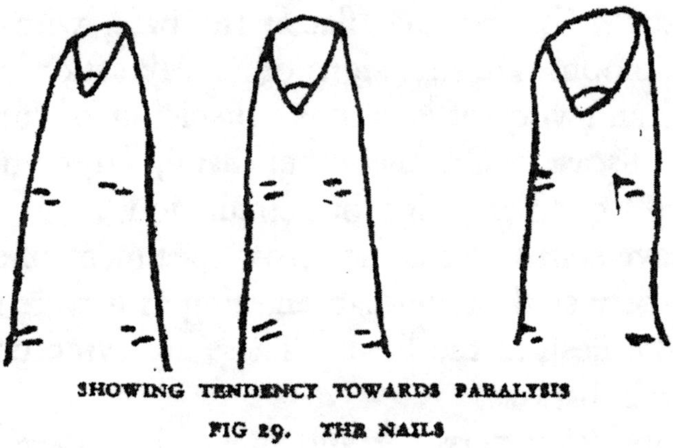

SHOWING TENDENCY TOWARDS PARALYSIS

FIG 29. THE NAILS

He seemed greatly relieved and withdrew with many thanks, after writing his name in my autograph book.

After completing a very successful tour through the United States, I returned for another season in New York.

One evening I was dining with a gentleman who was a great power in the financial world. Conversation turned on the strenuous life led by New York stockbrokers. He said casually:

"One needs a frame of iron and a brain of ice to stand the strain. Yesterday there was a tremendous flurry in 'steels,' caused by the manipulation of the Bet-you-a-Million Gates group. A friend of mine who had invested his all in these shares was so excited when they declined heavily that he dropped dead."

It was the gentleman who had called upon me haunted by the secret fear of sudden death.

Short nails, thin and flat at the base, with little or no moons, are sure signs of a weak action of the heart, and very often arouse suspicion of lurking heart disease. On the other hand, large moons denote a good and vigorous circulation.

I have sometimes come across specimens of short nails, very sunken and flat, entering as it were right into the flesh at the base. These are symptomatic of nerve diseases.

Short nails, very flat and inclined to curve out or lift up at the edges, are the fore-runners of paralysis, particularly if they are white and brittle as well as flat. If the latter is the case, the disease is more advanced.

As already stated, I had the honour of examining the lines and characteristics of the hands and nails of the late " Joe " Chamberlain. The line of Sun, or Success, was wonderfully well developed, but this was counter-balanced by the unmistakable indication of paralysis and sudden nerve collapse. As everybody knows, in the very zenith of his career, Joseph Chamberlain was stricken down into a complete invalid, compelled to live a life of inactivity until death released him. An almost similar case was that of Mr. Woodrow Wilson. The strain of his Success was too much for him. The very fact that he reached such a position of power was too great a burden for the brain, and the tragic failure of his physical powers was the prelude to a lingering death.

Short-nailed people have a greater tendency to suffer from heart-trouble, and from diseases affecting the trunk and lower limbs, than those with long nails.

Long-nailed persons are more exposed to troubles in the upper half of the system—the lungs, chest and head.

Natural spots on the nails have their message for those who can read them. Insignificant as they may seem, yet to the trained observer they carry their warning. When the nails are much flecked with these whitish spots, the whole nervous system requires a thorough overhauling. Too often they are the advance signs of a nervous breakdown.

Thin nails, if small, denote delicate health and want of energy. Nails that are very narrow and long, if high and much curved, threaten spinal trouble, and never promise great strength.

Not only do the nails show our bodily condition, they also indicate mental characteristics.

Long-nailed individuals are less critical and more impressionable than those with short nails, they are calmer in temper and more gentle. Usually they exhibit marked resignation under difficulties and trouble—they take things easily. On the other hand, small nails indicate ideality and denote an artistic nature; their possessors will be found to be fond of poetry, painting, and the fine arts.

I have often found that long-nailed people are visionary, and shrink from looking facts in the face —particularly if they are unpleasant.

Short-nailed individuals will be critical, and very practical. They are quick and sharp in judgment; they are fond of debate, and in an argument will hold out to the very last. They are sceptical of things they do not understand.

Nails shortened by the habit of biting, indicate the nervous and restless temperament.

The whole study of the characteristics of the nails of the hand is full of fascination. As I have pointed out, not only will conditions of health be indicated, but the mental characteristics as well.

CHAPTER XIII

SOME DIVERSE HANDS

WHEN taking up a study of the lines of the hand in relation to Life and Health, one cannot help being struck with the remarkable diversity of *shape*.

There is one point that I must always insist upon when reading the message of the hand—one cannot give an opinion upon a single line, without consideration of the whole; just as truly, one cannot pass judgment, as it were, upon an individual when considering the broad outline of this "marvellous member stamped with the impress of the Divine," as the great Dr. Abernethy termed the hand. Therefore it will be found of the greatest interest to consider the various kinds, or types, as they are called, into which the human hand is classified. These types have a close relationship to the lines we have been considering.

As the limbs of an animal differ in shape, colour and proportion, and by so doing denote breeding and hereditary peculiarities, so exactly do the hands and fingers of individuals. As the judge of a horse can tell from the shape of the limbs of the animal what one may expect through breeding, so may one be able to tell from peculiarities in the formation of a hand, what the individual owes to the Past.

There are seven accepted types of hands, corresponding in some measure to the seven races of Mankind. These divisions are important, and can be set out thus:

1. The Elementary, or lowest type,
2. The Square, or Useful hand,
3. The Spatulate, or Active, the Nervous hand,
4. The Knotty, or Philosophic hand,
5. The Conic, or Artistic type,
6. The Psychic, or Idealistic hand,
7. The Mixed hand.

Let us start by considering the first on this list—the Elementary hand (Fig. 30). It indicates with unerring accuracy the lowest type—in fact, on the border-lines between the Man and the Brute.

This type of hand is extremely short, thick-set, and clumsy. The thumb also is unusually short, and barely reaches the base of the first finger. I have always noticed that such a hand has very few lines upon it, seldom more than the three main ones of Heart, Head, and Life.

People possessing such a hand have little mental ability. They are violent in temper, but not brave; they have little or no control over their passions, and are brutal or animal in their desires.

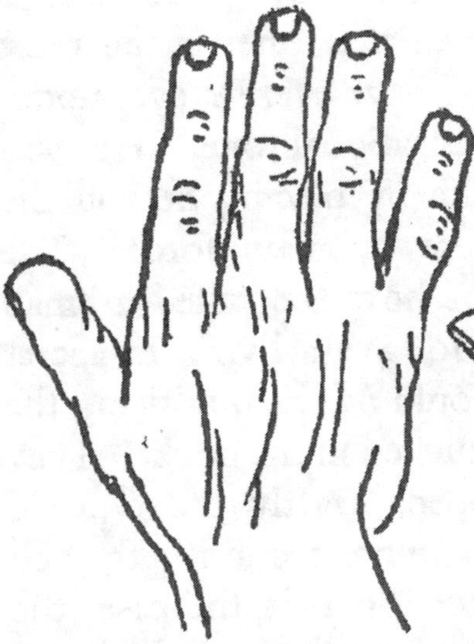

FIG. 30. THE ELEMENTARY HAND

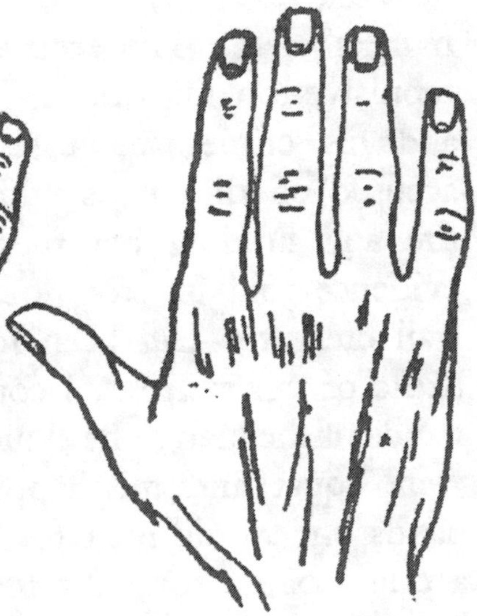

FIG. 31. THE SQUARE USEFUL HAND

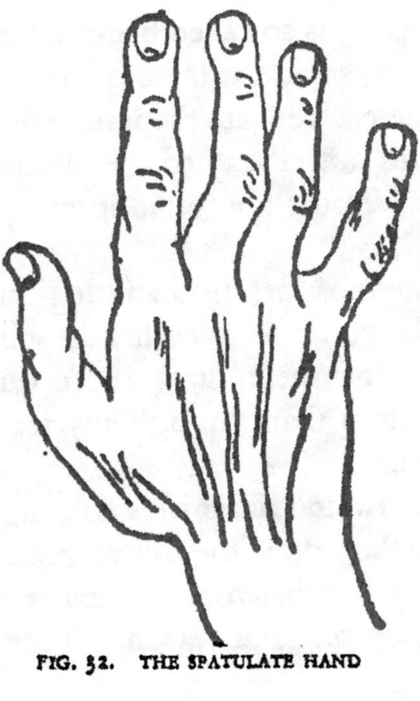

FIG. 32. THE SPATULATE HAND

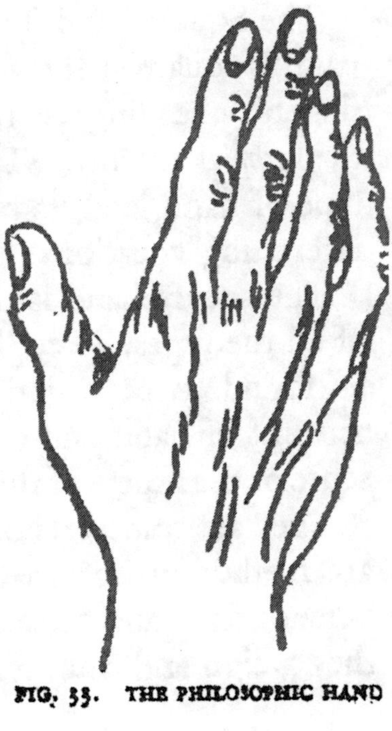

FIG. 33. THE PHILOSOPHIC HAND

While in Paris, I was taken by a friend to a murder trial. The accused was one of the most repulsive-looking ruffians I have ever set eyes upon, and his crime was a sensational one. He was accused of killing his wife by placing her on the fire and holding her there by main force. The evidence told its story of how the wife—a small frail creature—had been for years living in secret dread of this ruffian. I could not help noticing the hands of the man as he slouched in the dock. They were squat and misshappen, exactly the type of hands one would look for in connection with such a crime of horror. As too often is the case, the brutal man had possessed himself of a frail and delicate little wife.

The Square hand (Fig. 31) is so called because the palm is square at the wrist, square at the base of the fingers, the fingers themselves are square, particularly at the tips. This is well named the Useful type of hand, and its possessors are found in many interesting vocations.

The square hand is the most practical and logical of all the types. People who have such hands will be found to be orderly and methodical, more on account of habit and custom than through any real sense of the fitness of things.

They are respecters of law and order in a nation; are methodical in what they do; they have great perseverance and tenacity in what they undertake; they weigh and measure by rule and reason. They are sceptical in matters relating to ideality; they want logic for belief, and are extremely stubborn in their convictions.

In such a person we find little originality or imagination, but in work they have great force of application; hence they are usually successful.

Such people make good husbands or wives, for they are sincere and true in the promises they make——but they are not demonstrative in affection, and are often misunderstood.

Lawyers, doctors, and scientists, with captains of industry, usually have this type of hand. It will be found that their chief fault is that they worship Reason to the exclusion of the Idealistic. Thus they overlook much of the mystery of life, in their search for material success.

The Spatulate hand (Fig. 32) is usually crooked and irregular in outline, with the tips of each finger something like the spatula that chemists use in mortars. In other words, the extreme tip of the first joint of the finger will be wider than the base of that joint.

This type can be found with the palm itself spatulated, in two positions—either extremely broad at the base of the fingers and tapering towards the wrist; or very broad at the wrist and sloping towards the base of the fingers.

The spatulate hand may be either hard and firm, or soft and flabby. In the first-mentioned case, it indicates a nature restless and excitable, but full of energy of purpose and enthusiasm. In this case, it will be found to be a magnificent type to possess. It indicates intense love of action, energy, and independence of spirit; a love of invention, discovery, and originality.

Such hands are largely found among great navigators, explorers, discoverers, and also among engineers and mechanics.

But no matter in what condition of life these hands are found, they are remarkable for their independence of spirit, marked individuality, and their intense love of new ideas in doctrine, dogma, or civilization.

I have found these hands among men and women whom the world calls "cranks," just because they will not follow in the rut of conventionality or custom.

In considering the two variations of the palm itself, if the spatulate hand has the broad development at the base of the fingers, it is the more practical of the two. If such a man were an inventor, he would use his talents for more useful things of life; whereas if he had the broad development at the base of the hand, he would be inventive in the domain of idealism, and his inventions would not take the form of useful or practical things.

If this type of hand is found to be soft and flabby, it denotes a restless and irritable spirit. Such individuals are restless and changeable and can stick at nothing long—they lack continuity.

Perhaps of all types of hands, the knotty or philosophic is the most easily recognised (Fig. 33). It is long and angular, with bony fingers and heavily developed joints.

People possessing such hands have a marked personality distinct from individuals of other types. They are peculiar in habits, thoughts, and ideas.

They are philosophers in some form or another; friendly with all, yet they gain few associates. They seldom gain great success or wealth. They are students of Humanity, and often are great readers of character. They love neatness and order.

In character they are silent and secretive; often egotistical, through a belief in their own personality.

The tips of the fingers on a Philosophic hand may be either conic, square, or spatulate. In each case, the actions and ideas of the individual will largely be influenced by the peculiarities of the square, conic, or spatulate temperament.

The Conic or Artistic hand (Fig. 34) has often misled people on account of its name. An Artistic hand does not of necessity mean that the possessor is a painter or musician. It indicates a love of art, although people with artistic hands rarely carry out their ambitions. This hand is sometimes called "The Hand of Impulse." Artistic by temperament, these people do not wait to reflect, or use their own judgment. They are quick and clever in ideas, but they tire easily and lack concentration.

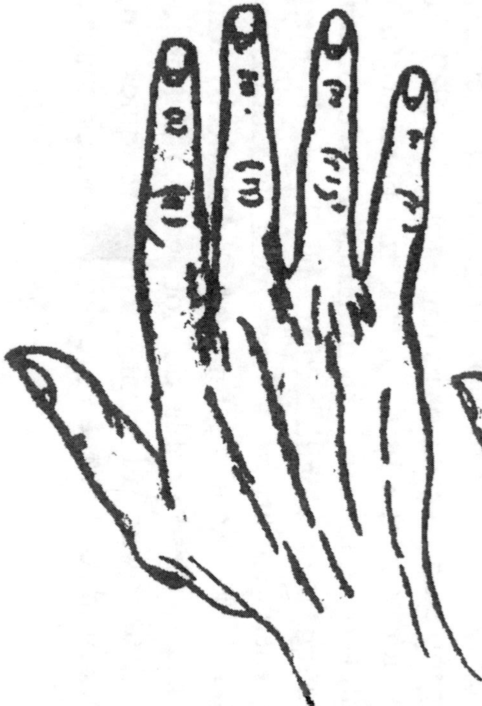

FIG. 34. THE CONIC OR ARTISTIC HAND

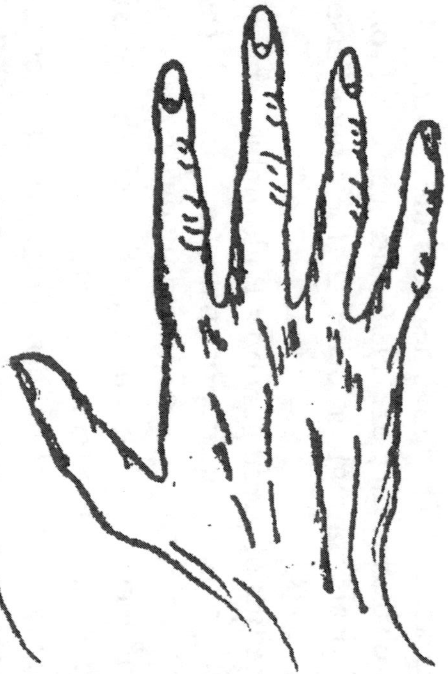

FIG. 35. THE PSYCHIC OR IDEALISTIC HAND

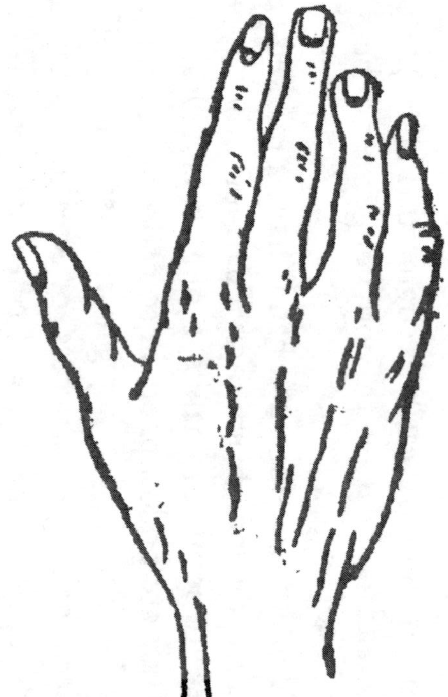

FIG. 36. THE MIXED HAND

They are, however, excellent conversationalists, and can grasp the drift of a subject quickly; they can learn almost anything, but they have not the real student's deep power of application.

Such people are easily offended over trifles; they are also impressionable to the people they meet.

Women with such hands love admiration to excess and are very susceptible to affairs of the heart. They cannot live without love, but they are the children of moods, and they must love very deeply before you can be certain of the constancy of their affection.

They are generous and sympathetic to a certain extent, when their personal comfort is not concerned. It is a better sign to find this type of hand firm and elastic, than full and flabby. In the latter case such people are selfish; they consider their own personal comfort and are indolent.

I now come to the Psychic hand (Fig. 35)—perhaps the most beautiful and unfortunate type of all, if judged from the point of view of worldly advancement. The pure type, however, is very rare, as modern civilization does not encourage the production of the temperament it foreshadows.

Its very formation indicates the helplessness of such hands to cling on to the skirts of life, or to grasp at opportunity as she passes by. Individuals with this class of hand have the purely visionary or idealistic nature; they usually spend half their days in the pursuit of some idea, and the other half in gathering up the lost threads in the web of life.

Individuals possessing psychic or pointed hands are very often extreme fanatics in religion and orthodox creeds, or else they use their devotional spirit in mysticism, and become devotees to fanciful ideas of occultism.

The Mixed hand (Fig. 36)—the last type to be considered—is the most difficult of all to describe. It is as if something of all the other types had been taken in order to build up this one. For example, the first finger might be found pointed, the second square, the third spatulate, and so forth. When such is the case, it denotes an individual full of versatility, but as changeable in purpose as the sands of the sea. Such a man would be adaptable to all sorts and conditions of ideas or circumstances, but erratic and uncertain in the use of his talents. A man with such a hand might play a little, sing a little, paint a little—but will rarely be great.

The mixed hand, in fact , belongs to the talented *dilettante*, who will never stick to anything long enough to become really great.

I may conclude these observations upon the types of hands by pointing out that, through the mixture of races, the pure or exact type of hand is rarely found. Hands are more often found containing two or three types together—the palm might be square, while the fingers might be pointed or philosophic ; or there might be three types together, as for example the palm square, the fingers near the palms and second joints philosophic, with the tips pointed or spatulated. If this is borne in mind, it will assist greatly in forming a more accurate opinion of the subject's character.

CHAPTER XIV

CONCLUSION

THOUGH we may never be able to penetrate the mystery of "How such things can be," that is no reason for saying that they are not possible. Just as it is impossible to solve the mystery of Life itself, so is it not possible to follow the meaning of all its various manifestations.

Every day investigators stumble upon some new truth, but in the investigation of that which concerns the Soul side of Life, the mystery may be all the greater, but none the less true.

Life, Purpose and Design are so intimately woven together by the loom of Destiny that our earthly eyes may well be satisfied if they but see the pattern—and no more.

One thing is certain—the occult side of life is the real life that, like a thread of gold, binds all together. It finds its expression in shapes and forms and lines, uses nations as the servants of its purpose, and nothing can escape the destiny of being part of the purpose of Life—whatever that purpose may be.

Occultism is the one Religion in whose Temple all may meet, where Catholic and Protestant,

Mohameddan or Hebrew may find something in common, in which they may trace the origin of their own ceremonial, and know the reason why such ceremonial was made by those whose footsteps have long been lost in the dust of centuries.

The Hebrew would find in it why the number Twelve was selected as the number of his Tribes, and the Christian would see the same truth in the number of the Apostles.

The Temple of Solomon would no longer be a dumb pile of masonry, but a revelation of God's command to Moses on the Mount: "Be sure that thou makest it according to the pattern which I showed thee in the heavens."

To the Christian, the ceremonial of his religion would be explained, while even the consecration service of a Catholic cathedral would assume an occult importance little guessed at by the priests who carry out the ceremony. Thus we have the Twelve crosses emblematic of the Twelve houses of the Zodiac; the Seven candles representing the Seven creative planets—seven being the spiritual number in all Creation; the Four crosses drawn on the Four corner-stones of the year; the Four signs of the season, and so on.

The thirty-three years' ministry of Christ, corresponding to a Solar cycle, with His crucifixion at a certain hour and on a certain day of the week, would no longer appear to be accidental, if read by the only Key which can and does unravel such things.

Under these conditions, Religion would become a living force, and not the intangible maze of ceremonies that it is to-day.

It was never the purpose of the Creator that men and women should be the unhappy beasts of burden that they are to-day, instead of the contented fellow-workers of His Infinite Purpose. Time is as nothing in the eyes of the Eternal, so it takes centuries for man to learn the story of his creation—the story that is written in all things—the last story that man ever reads.

Faith is the first-born of God, the heir that neither time nor tears can dispossess, and so in the end will occult knowledge possess the earth—and "the crooked ways shall be made straight."

The usefulness of Occultism lies in its strength to withstand the trials of daily life, its faith in the unfolding of God's purpose, its patience to wait the appointed time.

Such are a few of the reasons that prompt me to send this volume on its way. It may interest those who have already studied such subjects, while those who have not may be led to examine such questions for themselves, and so swell the ever increasing band of men and women who stem the tide of Materialism, and prevent humanity from forgetting that the Mystery of the World is still the visible—not the invisible.

FINIS